CW01081155

Here are nearly 200 'undiscovered' antiques, from Aeronautica to Zarfs, displayed in words and pictures for those who search for original collectables – *and* profit from them – on a small budget.

In junk shops and attics, in potting sheds, in grandparents' kitchens, in bottom drawers, on market stalls, in business premises – *everywhere* things are lying about neglected and waiting to be recognised for what they are : finely made objects which will never be manufactured again. They are old and rare and beautiful perhaps, and one of the purposes of this fascinating book is to confer upon a selection of them the status of 'antique'.

Peter Whittington, an avid junk rummager as well as antiques correspondent, presents bargain hunters with some alluring names to remember and look out for : Billies and Charleys, Brothel tickets, Distaffs, Love tokens, Mote skimmers, Moustache cups, Standishes, Trivets and many, many more.

Readers are invited to write to Peter Whittington, care of his Publishers, with their suggestions of further 'undiscovered antiques' for inclusion in a sequel volume.

Discovered by
PETER WHITTINGTON

Undiscovered Antiques

Garnstone Press

73-291342

UNDISCOVERED ANTIQUES
is published by
The Garnstone Press Limited
59 Brompton Road, London SW3 1DS

ISBN : 0 85511 080 5

Printed in Great Britain by
A. Wheaton and Company, Exeter

Contents

6

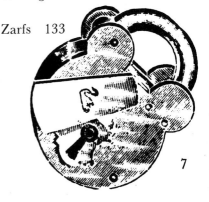

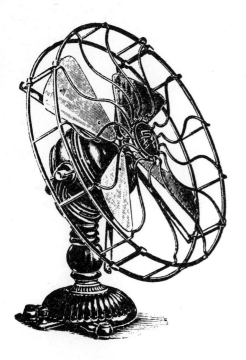

Introduction

Man is by nature a hoarder and collector of things; the desire to accumulate objects which may or may not have utilitarian value is very old and odd! Indeed, why should we not suppose that men in the Stone Age hoarded animal bones and stones of unusual shape purely for the fun of it. Pre-historians may say that the presence of these objects indicate a belief in the hereafter, or that they were tools and weapons, ornaments and dress required to equip the deceased in his new situation; but perhaps the old familiar objects were treasured so much that they had to accompany the corpse to its grave.

Few people nowadays would insist on their collections and material possessions being interred with them – yet the primeval assurance which seems to come from the possession of objects survives to this day. Of course the most obvious things which are collected are those which have an intrinsic value – gold, silver and precious jewels. Yet they are only valuable because very many people think so; and this is true also for most other collectables. Works of art may be chosen for their beauty, but some expensive postage stamps have little or no aesthetic appeal. In the case of antiques their desirability may be enhanced because they exhibit fine craftsmanship, or because they are rare, unusual or merely of great age.

The subjects and objects in this book might appear to have little to commend them therefore to the would-be collector, and this explains why they are happily 'undiscovered' . . . well, none of these objects is 'undiscovered' in the strictest sense, since some of them are being collected at this moment. The fun is that they are not the sorts of things which most people would regard as collectable. The reaction, when I remind my friends what is now being collected, is usually 'Coat hangers? Sand buckets? How ridiculous!'

As the stock of traditional collectables dries up and prices continue to rise, more and more collectors are snooping around in the back of junk shops looking for objects which they fondly imagine have not attracted the attention of their rivals. I am sadly aware that, in publishing this book, I am doing these lone wolves a grave disservice. There are a few objects which particularly interest me, and I am keeping very quiet about these for the time being; if your own particular thing or topic happens to be absent from these pages, then the chances are that it is because I am actively engaged in the field myself! But anyway, please let me have suggestions, care of my publishers, for the next book of undiscovered antiques. Then we can all make some money when we sell.

In presenting this list of nearly two hundred objects I have applied several criteria. I have scoured flourishing antique supermarkets, small antique and junk shops and taken careful notes of the offerings. One example of an article (which may have appeared on an antique stall accidentally) does not necessarily mean that it is collectable, and in each case the class of object has been seen by me several times over. There is always the possibility, of course, that objects find their way into the general antique market more in hope than to supply a demand; so there may be some borderline cases which have crept into this book because I have seen quite a number of them for sale. Another criterion which I have applied is their presence in the 'Wanted' and 'For Sale' columns in the collectors' magazines and periodicals.

The British Antique Dealers' Association defines an antique as an object produced before the year 1830, and they apply this definition to the material in which their members deal and which they are allowed to display for sale at the Annual Antiques Fair held at Grosvenor House, London. Legally, however, an antique is usually defined as any object which is at least one hundred years old, and this is the definition used by Customs and Excise in many countries. While a fair proportion of the objects in this book are over a hundred years old the majority are more recently made; yet for all practical purposes they are of course as antique in the eyes of most people as anything pertaining to the eighteenth century!

Perhaps we need a new definition of the word 'antique', in these days of built-in obsolescence. In *Undiscovered Antiques* I have tried where possible to explain why objects with which we were once so familiar have now vanished from everyday use. One could therefore say, with some justification, that an antique is anything rendered obsolete by changing fashions, morals and manners, or by advances in manufacturing technology. Ink pots – and even fountain pens – may be regarded as antique because so many of us prefer to use a ball-point pen; stud boxes are antique because most men now prefer 'collar-attached' shirts; coal scuttles are antique, or rapidly becoming so, as central heating advances in popularity; suspenders or garter clips are antique, because tights are fashionable and stockings virtually delights of the past. With

10

a little imagination and much energy the collector of tomorrow's antiques can probably discover many more objects once common and now hardly ever encountered. To keep one jump ahead of the field, for satisfaction (and, maybe, profit), it is necessary to be aware of changing fashions or modes of living before they have become established. Keep watching – good hunting!

Peter Whittington

Aeronautica

This is a vast field – and of far greater antiquity than most people realise. For instance, Leonardo's fifteenth century sketch of an ornithopter would come under the heading of aeronautica. In the late eighteenth century, when the ballooning craze was at its height, objects of all kinds were decorated with balloons – balloons ascending, descending or just sailing serenely across the countryide. Among the highly desirable items which turn up occasionally in the sale-rooms are watches, clocks, fan-leaves, enamel boxes, snuff boxes and even furniture decorated with balloon motifs. The majority of items associated with aeronautics, however, date from the invention of heavier-than-air machines. Among objects worth considering are vintage aircraft models, airline badges and insignia, uniforms and equipment of air crew, medals and badges of air forces, examples of airmail 'first flight' covers and postcard souvenirs of aviation meetings, posters advertising air races and similar events, actual parts of aircraft, objects with an aviation motif, airline timetables and brochures, aerial propaganda leaflets and other examples of 'psychological warfare'.

Almanacs

Books or tables containing a calendar of the days, weeks and months of the year and a register of saints' days and astronomical data became popular at the end of the fifteenth century, but they had their origins in the Roman *fasti* and the astrological tables of the ancient Egyptians. Blocks of wood with notches along their edges corresponding to the days of the year were known as clogg almanacs. They were of Scandinavian origin and were in use in some parts of England as late as the seventeenth century. *Old Moore's Almanac*, still published annually in Britain, was first published by Francis Moore in 1700 as *Vox Stellarum* (the voice of the stars) and contained predictions for 1701. Later almanacs were year books of statistical tables and general knowledge in a handy form.

13

Benjamin Franklin's fortune was founded in *Poor Richard's Almanack*, first published in 1732 and produced annually for over a quarter of a century. The *American Almanac and Repository of Useful Knowledge* was published at Boston from 1828 to 1861. *The Old Farmer's Almanac*, still in progress, has been published for many years. The *British Almanac* first appeared in 1828 while *Whitaker's Almanac*, still in progress, first appeared in 1868. In France the *Almanack Royal* first appeared in 1679, later became *Imperial* and is now *National*, reflecting the political changes of that country. Germany produced a number of almanacs, of which the best known, the *Almanack de Gotha* (first published in 1763) gives details of the royal and princely families of Europe as well as the usual statistical material.

Alphabet plates and mugs

In Victorian times, it seems, it was never too early to begin the task of educating infants and young children. A relatively painless way of instilling at least one of the three R's was to give the child plates and mugs adorned with the letters of the alphabet. These alphabet plates were very popular from about 1880 until World War One. The letters were usually arranged round the edge of the plate and the front and back were embellished with pictures. In fact alphabet plates were in existence about fifty years earlier and seem to have originated in the potteries of the English Midlands. The idea spread to the United States about 1875 and remained in vogue until about 1920. An extension of the alphabet idea was a plate bearing numerals or a plate with Biblical texts or proverbs of an 'improving' nature. Though plates are the commonest form of crockery, decorated cups and mugs were also given the alphabet treatment. Occasionally a complete set of matching plate, cup and saucer may turn up. Alphabet plates are sometimes found in glass, pewter or enamelled tinware, but earthenware was the commonest material used.

Andirons

These were iron bars, in pairs, on which logs were laid for burning in an open fireplace. They stood on short legs and were usually connected with an upright guard, giving them the grotesque appearance of a dog (hence the term fire-dogs). This guard, being a very conspicuous feature, was invariably the subject of lavish decoration with figures, animals, flowers and heraldic emblems. Most andirons were constructed of wrought iron but sumptuous examples in gilded bronze are also known. Relatively plain andirons were used in kitchens, with ratcheted uprights for the spits.

Apple scoops

These objects properly belong within the realm of folk-art, despite their mundane purpose. They were carved out of wood or bone and may be recognised by their spatulate shaft ending in a series of knobs, like knuckles. The shaft was often engraved with a date and sets of initials, indicating that the scoop had been given by some young swain to his lady love as a token of their betrothal. These quaint articles were to the English what the carved loving-spoons (q.v.) were to the Welsh. This attractive custom seems to have died out in the mid-nineteenth century, though it may survive in remote country districts to this day for all I know. Carved apple scoops turn up occasionally in provincial junk-shops.

Apprentice pieces

Occasionally one comes across pieces of furniture in miniature – not the very tiny items which were intended for dolls' houses but something like the real thing on a small scale. Such pieces were more than likely the work of apprentices, either while practising the arts of carpentry, joinery and cabinet-making, or as a 'masterpiece', a test piece produced at the end of the apprenticeship. Chairs, tables, chests of drawers and beds are the commonest examples of these apprentice pieces, but I remember once seeing a splendid example of a miniature grand piano, measuring little more than a foot across and six inches high. Often mistaken for apprentice pieces are miniature items produced as a sales gimmick. They include working models or small-scale versions of products and were used by travelling salesmen to demonstrate their companies' wares. Miniaturised reproductions of this sort are still being made, mainly to show their paces at exhibitions and trade fairs, often in a limited space. Whether they are apprentice pieces or demonstration models is almost irrelevant; both types have a definite appeal to the collector in these days of cramped house-room.

Argyles

These gravy warmers are said to have been named after the fourth Duke of Argyll who is credited with inventing them, but it now seems likely that similar devices were in use at a much earlier date. Admittedly they became popular in the second half of the eighteenth century, so perhaps the Duke did have something to do with it. The argyle is a purely British phenomenon. The majority of examples now in existence are of silver and the period of their popularity coincided with the great era of the Georgian and Regency silversmiths. It is interesting to note that argyles were also produced in tin-glazed delftware and Wedgwood creamware. They may be recognised by their inner compartment which held the gravy, the outer 'jacket' containing hot water. Less common were silver or Sheffield plate argyles with a central compartment intended for a bar of heated iron.

Ash trays

Ashtrays rank among the more collectable objects on account of their small size and great diversity. They began to appear about the middle of the nineteenth century when cigarette smoking overtook pipe smoking in popularity and became more acceptable in public by both sexes. Stylistically they range from plain rectangles stamped out of heavy sheet brass to the ornate table ash trays which incorporated match stands and pipe racks. They have been produced in almost every material, though pottery, porcelain, glass, brass and bronze are the commonest. Tobacco companies and breweries were quick to realise the potential of the ash tray as a medium for advertising their products. Countless different varieties of these advertising ash trays have been produced all over the world in the past eighty years, offering limitless scope to the collector. The ash tray also inspired the manufacturers of souvenirs and novelties, and this industry continues unabated to this day. Novelty ash trays range from the whimsical to the impudent, from the naïve to the frankly risqué, decorated with nude or scantily clad young ladies. Ash trays in the form of miniature chamber pots inscribed 'Park your weary ash' typify the low humour of this genre. Pocket ash trays, in the form of miniature warming pans, are also worth looking for.

Baby rattles

It is not known who was the genius who discovered the power of the rattle to calm the fretful infant, but he must have lived a very long time ago, since baby rattles in various forms are known from Greek and Roman times, if not earlier. They come in a fantastic variety of forms and shapes, their only common feature being that they are hollow and contain tiny balls which cause the rattle. Many of them take the form of little dolls, in all kinds of material from terra cotta to plastic, from silver and gold to brass or pewter. Often they incorporated a teething ring, the early examples being made of bone, ivory or even mother-of-pearl. Decoration in brightly painted enamel showed fairy tale characters or included snatches of popular nursery rhymes. A collection of baby rattles of the past hundred and fifty years alone would provide an interesting commentary on the social history of the period. Some rattles of the past eighty years also incorporated whistles and tiny bells. Novelty rattles from the turn of the century were shaped like animals; cats, dogs and the new-fangled teddy bear were popular subjects.

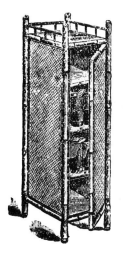

Bamboo furniture

In the 1860s and 1870s there was a tremendous craze for anything Japanese in appearance. One manifestation of this was the great popularity of flimsy bamboo furniture, which reached its peak about 1875. This material was particularly suited to bedroom furniture, but in its hey-day it was also used for drawing-room pieces – tables and sideboards. It was economical, since the basic materials were cheap and the methods of construction relatively straightforward. It was often combined with fine basket or cane work, and sometimes in conjunction with wood (e.g. table tops and the panels in desks and cabinets). The result was often light and pleasing and surprisingly strong. Although the vogue for this furniture declined towards the end of the century, it never quite died out. It has recently returned to favour and, while not quite strong enough to be a commercial proposition, it has caught the fancy of the collector. Thus pieces which a few years ago were quite unsaleable now have a definite market value. Originally the bamboo was left in its natural honey-brown state, but in the revival of interest it has become fashionable to paint it.

Barbed wire

Twisted strands of wire with small barbs at regular intervals were invented over a century ago in France, but it was in the rapidly expanding West of the United States that barbed wire came into its own. The first American wire was produced in 1873 by Henry Rose but shortly afterwards Jacob Haish and Joseph Glidden also entered the market with similar products. In the intervening century some four hundred different types of barbed wire have been manufactured, differing in the gauge of the wire and in the size and composition of the barbs. The association of barbed wire with the romance of the Old West is so strong that collecting strands of various types has grown into one of the major hobbies in the United States. More than 150,000 collectors are said to be active and there are several dealers in 'antique' barbed wire, mainly in the western states where examples of the older varieties can still be picked up along the country roads. The wire is known by many colourful names – Meriweather's Snake, Kittleston's Half-Hitch, Merrill Twirl and Glidden Two Point are typical examples. Barbed wire is best collected in foot lengths mounted on sticks or boards.

Bayonets

If swords and daggers have now been priced out of the market, the collector of edged weapons can still find a great deal of scope in the humbler bayonet. No one is really sure of the origins of this weapon, though it may be named after the French town of Bayonne. The earliest bayonets were no more than knives rammed into musket muzzles as a last resort when reloading was impossible and close-quarter fighting inevitable. The British Army first used them at the Battle of Killiecrankie (1689) and its defeat at the hands of the Jacobites is attributable to the inexperience of the red-coats in fixing their bayonets. Plug bayonets were in use on the continent of Europe a decade earlier. The plug bayonet, which fitted into the muzzle, was the earliest type, but was superseded in the eighteenth century by the appropriately named sword bayonet. These had a sword grip and a socket into which the muzzle of the firearm could be fitted. Thereafter countless variations and modifications in the socket-bayonet have appeared all over the world, some with broad or narrow blades, others with spikes, a few with saw-blades or trowel-blades. Quite a lot of them were surprisingly decorative (particularly the bayonets used in Nazi Germany). Even in this nuclear age, the bayonet is still part of the equipment of the infantryman.

Bee smokers

These gadgets were used by apiarists in order to quieten or round up their bees. The technique of tranquillising bees by smoking them out is of great antiquity, but these patent devices date from the late nineteenth century. They consisted of a metal container with attached bellows. Smouldering rags were placed in the container and smoke produced by working the bellows. The containers (known as 'stoves') came in various sizes and shapes. Brass or copper bee smokers, brightly polished, have been converted for use as flower holders.

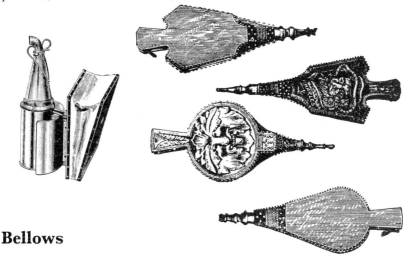

Bellows

Americans call these appliances blowers, which is a more aptly descriptive term. The word, still common in Britain, traces its ancestry to the Old English *blastbaelig* – blow-bag. This became corrupted to 'bellies' (bags) but by the sixteenth century 'bellows' was in use. Some form of the bellows has been recorded from pre-Christian times in Egypt, while the goatskin bellows of India and China, used to this day, are probably of comparable antiquity. European bellows, in use since the Middle Ages, consist of two flat boards (usually heart-shaped) joined round their edges by a wide band of leather to enclose an air chamber. An inlet valve is let into the lower board and air is expelled through a narrow tube. Domestic bellows, for fanning a reluctant fire into flames, were often quite decorative. The boards were carved or inlaid with brass, and the handles and outlet nozzle were also ornamented in various ways. Flowers or even scenery could be painted on the outer side of the boards. Modern grates and improved flues did away with the need for bellows by World War One and they gradually fell into disuse.

Bentwood furniture

Early in the nineteenth century Michael Thonet, of Boppard in the Rhineland, discovered that wood could be bent and shaped by the action of steam and high pressure. Under the patronage of Prince Metternich he established a factory at Vienna for the production of bentwood furniture. The chairs, tables and even beds which Thonet manufactured were almost revolutionary in design and clean lines, antedating the tubular steel furniture of the present day. Bentwood, like wicker furniture (q.v.) was especially popular for gardens and conservatories, but was also used in cafés and restaurants. Bentwood furniture gradually went out of fashion in the years before World War Two, but is now enjoying something of a revival. It is still quite plentiful in second-hand furniture shops and junk shops, not yet having been promoted to the status of antique. The best buys are rocking chairs, sofas and tables, especially if the bentwood exhibits intricate patterns or construction.

Berlin wool work

A type of embroidery which became very popular in the latter half of the last century. A picture or design was stencilled on to a piece of canvas and the picture built up with short thrums of brightly coloured wool, using a rug-making technique. The resulting picture, when newly completed, had a rich, thick-piled quality. Although many examples found today have faded as a result of exposure to sunlight they were otherwise very durable and may be found in good condition. Flowers, birds, historical and biblical motifs, even attempts at portraiture, formed the subjects of these pictures. They were mounted on firescreens, used as cushion covers, or framed in glass and hung on walls. Attempts have been made in recent years to revive the art of the wool picture and one can now buy stencilled sheets and kits. The resulting pictures are rather stereotyped and their value to the collector of the future is problematical. Berlin wool work died out before World War One, but the best examples date from the period 1880–1900.

Bidets

Toilet fixtures of this type are still comparatively rare in Britain and America though they have long been an indispensable feature of bathrooms on the continent of Europe. Although these items of sanitary hardware (designed for washing the feet, the more intimate parts of the body, or soaking one's smalls overnight) include turn-of-the-century examples with elegant Art Nouveau moulding or elaborate underglaze decoration, the chief interest from the point of view of the collector lies in the portable bidets which pre-date the water closet by centuries. The Victoria and Albert Museum in London possesses at least one attractive bidet of porcelain contained in an ornately carved case and stand with matching seat cover. Small bidets in earthenware, copper, brass or hardwood are also known, from the seventeenth century onwards. The more decorative types can easily be converted for house plants and since they were not plumbed in they can be sited in any part of one's house.

Biedermeier

This is a composite word describing a style in applied art which was fashionable in the period from 1830 to 1860 in Germany and Austria. The word was coined from Biedermann and Bummelmeier, two magazine characters used to satirise the philistinism of Central European petit bourgeoisie. The rapid rise of the new middle class in Europe in the mid-nineteenth century stimulated the production of furniture, silver, porcelain and glass. The new techniques of mechanisation and mass production had their repercussions on the applied arts. Although, inevitably, there was much which was poor in craftsmanship and design, there were also many examples of fine workmanship. It was fashionable to decry the florid character of Biedermeier and condemn it as a whole, but discerning collectors have long realised that many examples of the genre are worth preserving. In furniture, dressers, sideboards, wardrobes, settles and easy chairs offer considerable scope, but there is also a great deal that is of interest to be found among the rather heavy and ornate porcelain tableware and centre-pieces, the cut-glass bowls and vases and the enormous silver presentation pieces of the period.

Billies and Charleys

Two mid-nineteenth century beachcombers, William Smith and Charles Eaton, who made a precarious living on the mudflats of the Thames estuary, once discovered a fifteenth century medal which they disposed of to the British Museum for a considerable sum. Inspired by this piece of luck they began to manufacture spurious antiquities – figures, goblets, medals and weapons – which they cast from an alloy of copper and lead popularly known as cock metal. For a short time they succeeded in deceiving a number of collectors, but inevitably they were unmasked. How they ever succeeded in their fraud is a mystery since their manufactures were incredibly naïve and full of mistakes. Their medals, for example, bore nonsensical gibberish instead of correct Latin inscriptions and their methods of applying dates to objects were perfectly risible. With singular perversity, however, people will persist in collecting 'billies and charleys' as these impostures are known. It has been estimated that they could have produced fewer than 1000 objects; yet the number of items attributed to them today is far in excess of that figure. And now it is virtually impossible to distinguish a genuine billie from a 'billie' billie!

Bird cages

The keeping of caged birds became popular in Western Europe in the eighteenth century and it is from that period that elegant cages date. The cheaper cages were fashioned from wood and are relatively plain in workmanship. However, to blend in with the décor of the eighteenth century drawing-room or *salon* beautiful cages in gilt metal were produced. The cages and their stands were often elaborately decorated with enamel, ormolu and other expensive materials. Even the accessories rank as collector's pieces – seed trays of silver and water containers in fine decorated porcelain were by no means uncommon. Nineteenth century bird cages were more functional, yet managed to incorporate a certain degree of ornament. Many of the plain metal cages and stands have survived and, given a fresh coat of white enamel paint, are still giving good service while looking decorative at the same time.

Biscuit tins

Some time ago an acquaintance of mine took his deceased father's coin collection to a dealer in the hope of selling it. The dealer was unimpressed by the motley accumulation of coins – but was sufficiently interested in the tin box which housed it to purchase the collection for £5. The box was an attractive biscuit tin of the 1890s, decorated in the Art Nouveau style of that period with floral motifs stamped on the lid. Biscuit tins in unusual shapes – octagons, hearts or animal 'novelty' format – were popular before World War Two, but are becoming increasingly hard to find. Even the more prosaic rectangular tins are worth collecting if the decoration and inscriptions are reasonably intact. Biscuit tins advertising long-forgotten brands appeal to the nostalgia in collectors. Particularly desirable are those tins which were produced for commemorative purposes. In this category come the boxes celebrating Queen Victoria's Diamond Jubilee (1897) and various Coronations from 1902 onwards. Tins which contained biscuits or confectionary sent to troops in the Boer War and World War One often had a patriotic motif and are now sought by collectors of militaria.

Blotters and blotter-holders

In the days before quick-drying ink became popular the blotter was a very necessary piece of office equipment. Most blotters consisted of semi-circles of wood with blotting paper mounted on the curved face and a metal back and handle on the flat side. The blotter was rocked over the still wet ink. Blotters vary enormously in style and decoration, from very plain wooden ones to those beautifully ornamented with silver scrolls and curlicues. They may also be found with marquetry decoration, or lacquered with mother-of-pearl inlays. A few blotters were constructed on an all-metal principle, usually brass, but sometimes silver.

Blotter-holders were usually quarto-sized 'books' whose pages consisted of sheets of blotting paper. Examples of these, bound, and with sheets in contrasting colours, were sold for a few pence around 1900, but in pristine condition they are now scarce. The covers ranged from decorated leather to stout card, the latter often having a coloured picture mounted on the front. The more expensive leather covers sometimes had silver clasps and mounts, and these are now highly desirable.

Boiserie

This is a collector's term to describe the application of decorative techniques to wood. The principal source of boiserie is the carved wood panelling from old country houses. Demolition and redevelopment of these sites has brought to light a great deal of these decorative pieces and they are now finding an appreciative setting in modern homes. Even quite small pieces of panelling are being utilised as wall decoration. The dating of boiserie is often difficult since reproductions of medieval and renaissance styles were popular in the late nineteenth century. Jacobean panelling, not only from walls and partitions but also from chests, cupboards and dressers, turn up from time to time. Quite often a piece of furniture as a whole may be beyond repair or preservation but the decorative panels can be salvaged for use as ornaments in their own right.

26

Bookmarks

A second-hand bookseller of my acquaintance used to keep a small stock of bookmarks – to give away to children as a gesture of goodwill. One day he woke up to the fact that many of these items were worth collecting and that there was a ready market for them. The most desirable type of bookmark is in woven silk, made on the same technique as the Stevengraph silk picture. At one time bookmarks were given as prizes in Sunday schools to children who had learned their biblical texts correctly. As a rule these items had biblical themes and were inscribed with appropriate mottoes and texts. The earliest bookmarks of this type date from 1854 when Charles Stevens diversified his silk weaving business from hat-ribbons to something more profitable. Apart from the biblical ones there were literary bookmarks, embellished with characters from Shakespearean plays or contemporary novels and quotations from the great masters of English literature. Stevens also produced bookmarks featuring early locomotives, while ballooning scenes are now popular with collectors of aeronautica (q.v.). Thin ivory bookmarks with silver mounts were fashionable at the turn of the century and still turn up from time to time. Of lesser interest, but still worth collecting, are examples in card with chromolithographed pictures.

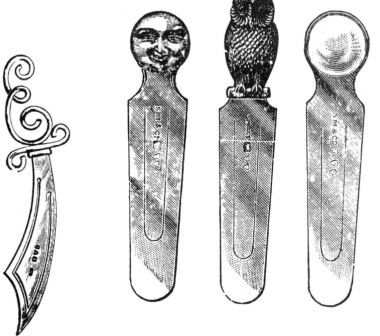

Boots and shoes

Leather is amazingly indestructible, and examples of leather footwear dating back thousands of years have been preserved in reasonably good condition. As feet have not changed over the centuries (except to become longer and broader) it would be logical to assume that boots and shoes have altered little over the years. But the caprices of fashion are such that an amazing variety of footwear has evolved, even in comparatively recent times. Collectors' interest naturally centres on the more decorative examples, in leather or cloth of different colours, ornamented with silver buckles. Among the more prosaic types, the footwear used by different armies appeals to militaria enthusiasts. The footwear adapted by primitive peoples all over the world offers immense scope, from the wooden clogs of the Netherlands (often richly painted) to the moccasins of the American Indians. Little more than a century ago the natives of St. Kilda, off the Scottish coast, used the skin from the neck and head of the gannet as shoes – though usually they preferred to go barefoot. Sales of costume (q.v.) by the major auctioneers invariably include boots and shoes, the majority dating from the eighteenth century.

Bottle openers

Chronologically, bottle openers came much later than corkscrews, dating from the beginning of the century when metal caps for sealing bottles came into use. Originally they were known as cap removers – a term liable to give rise to considerable confusion! The ordinary utilitarian bottle opener has not changed in shape over the years. From the collector's point of view, however, the chief interest in bottle openers lies in the many 'novelty' shapes which incorporate figures of sportsmen, drunken topers, nude ladies and so on. For the purist there are beautifully decorated bottle openers with silver handles and jewelled mounts.

Brackets

Metal brackets of various kinds have been in use for centuries, but for the collector the most interesting ones are the decorated types popular in the last century. Cast- or wrought-iron brackets, with openwork decoration of floral or geometric designs were popular for many years and fine examples are still plentiful. The more elaborate ones often incorporated animal or human figures. Be on the look-out for the late nineteenth century brackets decorated with the tendrils and sinuous lines characteristic of Art Nouveau; these are now very much in demand. The range of brackets is enormous. The commonest type was designed to support shelves but one will also find brackets for stair rods, curtains, door screens and window screens, gas mantles, oil lamps and wall lanterns. Large ornamental brackets were provided on wash stands and lavatory cisterns, often with whimsical designs of fishes, dolphins and other marine life. At the other extreme are the delicate candle brackets, usually in brass, which were fitted to pianos. When the pianos were modernised and streamlined the brackets were usually discarded, so nowadays they are becoming quite hard to find.

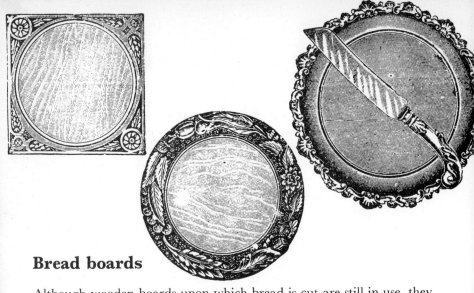

Bread boards

Although wooden boards upon which bread is cut are still in use, they are becoming less common in these days of sliced, wrapped loaves, and some of them make very nice collector's pieces. Many bread boards are simply circles or rectangles of wood, but it was inevitable that Victorian predilection for the ornamental should result in some very attractive examples with intricately carved borders. However, the finest and most unusual decorative boards come from Europe, where ready sliced bread does not yet have a very firm hold.

Brothel tickets

The Roman poet Martial (Book VIII) refers to *Spintriae* or *Lasciva Nomismata* which may have been used as tickets of admission to Roman brothels. The motifs on these metal tokens were highly pornographic, indicating their purpose. Nearer the present day, however, tokens or tickets of bronze, brass, ivory or card have been produced for admission to brothels and bawdy houses in England, America and various European countries. The metal ones were probably given to clients as souvenirs of their visit, judging by the lewd inscriptions and erotic symbolism on them. Unfortunately many examples now in circulation are either forgeries or completely bogus, created to satisfy modern demand for the bizarre and the curious. More interesting in many respects are the cards, particularly of European origin, which were passed to tourists in Paris, Berlin, Budapest and other cities where prostitution was prevalent at the turn of the century. These cards, distributed by touts, advertised the attractions of various brothels and the services offered.

Buckles

These dress accessories date back to prehistoric times and have been collected for a very long time. Nevertheless there is still plenty of opportunity for the collector who concentrates on the more recent examples, particularly from the mid-nineteenth century onwards. Silver buckles for shoes, belts and sashes are already expensive, especially the earlier ones, or those bearing the mark of a famous silversmith. But there are plenty of gilt or silver-plated buckles from the turn of the century, ranging from elaborate openwork to relatively severe Art Nouveau designs, from those inlaid with semi-precious stones to more modest enamelled buckles. Among the smaller buckles may be mentioned those fitted to ladies' garters or gentlemen's braces (suspenders) and arm bands. Many of these, seventy or eighty years ago, were quite ornamental in design and are worth looking out for. Small buckles were also used on ladies' hats and veils and these were often shaped in the form of flowers, butterflies or birds.

Button hooks

In the days before World War One when ladies favoured high buttoned boots the button hook was indispensable. These versatile instruments were also used to do up gloves and gentlemen's stiff shirtfronts. Button hooks were often given away with purchases in shoe shops, but these were relatively plain and unlikely to be interesting for the collector unless they bear the name of the shop or the brand name of its products. Button hooks sold by haberdashers and even jewellers, however, were frequently decorated with mother-of-pearl handles, wood inlaid with brass or silver, or even solid silver shaped in the form of animals, birds, humans, flowers and trees. Some button hooks also incorporated knives and other gadgets in their handles. Even relatively plain wooden-handled hooks are worth considering as collectable items since the early examples were hand-turned and no two are quite alike. Glove hooks were generally smaller and less robust in appearance, but otherwise decorated in the same way as button hooks.

Cake moulds

Slabs of wood with pictures or patterns incised intaglio into the surface were popular in Europe for imprinting decoration on pastry, bread and cakes. These moulds may sometimes be found in earthenware or beaten copper but those carved in cherry or boxwood are the most desirable. Cake moulds were never very popular in Britain or America but are still to be found in Scandinavia and the Low Countries where they are being manufactured to this day. They come in a wide variety of shapes and sizes, and with various pictorial motifs.

Cake stands

Another good example of the decorative combined with the useful is the cake stand, which used to be an indispensable feature of afternoon tea in the drawing-room. The majority of cake stands combine craftsmanship in wood and metal with ceramics and glass, and the decorative treatment of this combination is infinitely varied. It is possible to find stands made entirely of wood, with three or more wooden platters held in wooden uprights. More often, however, the plates or trays will be of porcelain with silver or silver-plated surrounds and frames, held in a wooden or metal stand. The half century before World War One witnessed the production of many different types. To some extent, of course, they are still being produced, but the modern examples lack the ornamental appeal of the nineteenth century cake stands.

B

Can openers

The preservation of foodstuffs by canning is of surprising antiquity, dating from 1809 when François Appert, a Parisian confectioner, succeeded in preserving food in specially constructed bottles which had been kept in boiling water. Appert was awarded 12,000 francs by a grateful government. Curiously enough, a further fifty years elapsed before Pasteur was able to explain the principles of sterilisation by which canning was made feasible. Tin-coated steel containers were first used in the United States in 1839 (though the tin can was the invention of an Englishman, Peter Durand). It follows, therefore, that can openers date from the early 1840s. The simple steel blade set in a metal or wooden handle has been in use ever since, but the latter half of the nineteenth century saw the manufacture of numerous different types with fancy handles. The late Victorian can openers had richly ornamented handles in copper, brass, nickel or even silver. Others had animals' heads mounted above the cutting blade. Rotary can openers came into use in the early 1900s. Although various refinements in this type of opener have appeared they are basically of little interest to the collector.

Canes and cane handles

Canes, as a dress accessory for both ladies and gentlemen, have been fashionable on and off since the sixteenth century. Those belonging to the earliest period, down to the late seventeenth century, are comparatively rare and examples with ivory pommels decorated in piqué are now highly priced. Canes declined for several generations but came back in the second half of the eighteenth century when they became a necessity to ladies whose extremely high heels made walking both painful and unsteady. This was the period of greatest ornamentation, particularly in the handle, and great ingenuity and artistry were shown in devising unusual decorations. Birds, animals and mythological creatures were fashioned in gold, silver or even porcelain and mounted on the heads of canes. Small flasks containing spirits were cunningly incorporated in the handles of canes so that gentlemen could indulge in a quiet tipple. Another ingenious device dating from 1785 was the illuminated cane whose handle contained a candle and reflector to assist nocturnal perambulation.

See also Walking Sticks.

Car badges and mascots

The motor car has always borne a distinctive badge, ever since its inception in the 1880s. At a very early date the motor car must have become something of a status symbol, and this can be seen in the psychology of the badges and mascots with which cars are adorned. It is significant that many of those *marques* which have the highest reputation – Bugatti, Alvis, Rolls-Royce and Delage – were content with austere emblems consisting of names or initials only. At the other extreme, however, are the flamboyant badges of Hispano-Suiza, Rover, Maserati and the pre-war American Stutz. Many badges had a strong heraldic element ranging from the arms of Oxford on the Morris badge to the appropriately aristocratic arms of the kingdom of Württemberg used by Porsche. Junkyards and car 'cemeteries' are a fruitful source of these attractive items. Also worth collecting are the club badges fitted to radiator grilles. Quite a collection could be formed of the Automobile Association badges which have changed in style and material over the years. Mascots such as the Rolls-Royce silver lady, the Armstrong-Siddeley sphinx and the leaping jaguar, as well as decorated radiator caps, are another aspect of motoring memorabilia.

Carnets de bal

Slim cases containing cards on which ladies inscribed the names of their intended partners for each dance at the beginning of a ball. The cards served as an *aide memoire* to avoid the complication and embarrassment of double-booking. Often thin leaves of ivory were used instead and these had the advantage that they could be wiped clean and reused indefinitely. Carnets de bal were always decorative in appearance, in keeping with their elegant surroundings, and at their best would be sumptuously decorated with diamonds and rubies set in gold. More usually they were made of ivory, mother-of-pearl, polished hardwood, silver, leather or satin with a card base. Apart from the inscription 'Carnet de Bal' or 'Souvenir' which was often engraved on the cover, they may be recognised by their leaves. The upper third of the case was hinged at one side and lifted up to reveal the cards or leaves inside.

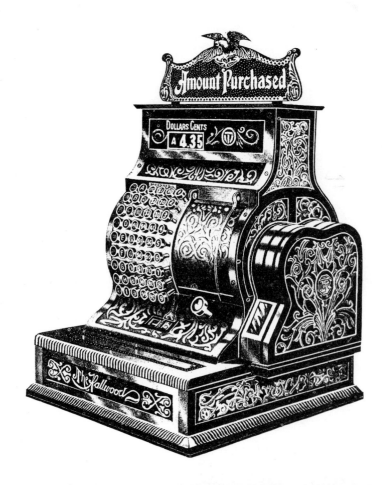

Cash registers

The earliest cash registers appeared in the mid-nineteenth century and consisted of a drawer fitted with wooden compartments for various denominations of coins, and a simple alarm till-lock attachment. Early registers are often beautiful examples of the carpenter's craft, constructed of oak, walnut or cherry, with fitted coin bowls. Towards the end of the century the security devices operating the till-lock became more elaborate and, at the same time, mechanism for recording the transactions was developed. Cash registers, incorporating such refinements as enumerators, total cash computers and receipt dispensers, cost £100 or more in 1900 and, as befitted such expensive pieces of equipment, much thought was given to their ornamentation. The impressive keyboard would be set in a handsome lacquered frame and the sides and back of the register would often be decorated with gilding or cast metal-work. Because of their bulkiness, however, old cash registers are relatively cheap today, particularly in Britain where the advent of decimal currency in recent years has rendered so many of them obsolete.

Casolettes

Originally these objects were designed as pastille burners, to sweeten the air and blot out the ubiquitous stench of the seventeenth century towns. The early examples were made of metal, usually copper, brass or iron. Gradually, however, the casolette was transformed in purpose (purely decorative) and material (mainly porcelain) though the basic urn shape remained with the perforated bowl through which the aromatic vapour was dispersed. Late eighteenth century casolettes became highly ornate, in marble with ormolu mounts, or in porcelain lavishly decorated and gilded. Casolettes were made chiefly in France and may be found in various styles from Louis Quinze to the late-Empire of the 1820s, running the whole gamut of baroque, rococo and neo-classical motifs. They were also produced in Germany and England in the same period, for use as ornaments (usually in matching pairs) on tables and mantelpieces.

Casters

Small containers for sugar have been in use for three centuries and form an interesting group of collectables in themselves. They were usually made of silver in cylindrical or baluster form, with a domed, gilded top perforated with holes. The perforation was often highly decorative in itself, either in patterns of round holes, diamond or foliate piercing. They are also found in Sheffield plate or silver-gilt and were sometimes produced in sets of three or more in differing sizes. A few rare examples are known in Chinese export porcelain based on European silver patterns. Rather similar in external appearance were muffineers and pounce pots (qq.v.) which served other purposes altogether.

Chamber pots

An apocryphal but widespread tale of the old American West concerned traders who sold chamber pots to the Indians who subsequently used them as food containers. This was related as an example of the laughable ignorance of the savage, but, in this day and age, when chamber pots are no longer in general use as originally intended, it is regarded as very trendy in American bars to use them as containers for pretzels, salted peanuts and stuffed olives! *Autre temps, autres moeurs*, indeed. A generation has now grown up which never knew this handy bedroom convenience, but fortunately there are still plenty of them around to provide the collector with an assortment of decorative styles at little cost. Chamber pots in pottery or porcelain with attractive floral or scenic decoration are still available for £2 to £5. Marked examples by the more famous potteries are likely to cost more. There is currently a fashion for plain chamber pots bearing the broad arrow of the British government and the royal monogram. One enterprising dealer was recently doing a brisk trade in these articles, claiming that they had come from Buckingham Palace. A rare pewter chamber pot was sold at Sotheby's in 1970 for £170: dating from about 1690 it had come from the wreck of the warship *Association* and was thought to have belonged to Admiral Sir Cloudesley Shovell.

Chatelaines

Until about 1914 it was customary for the lady of the house to wear a chain girdle from which were suspended various objects used in connection with her household duties. These chains were known as chatelaines and were usually manufactured in silver. At the centre of the chain was a large flat plate from which the smaller chains and objects were suspended and it was this plate which was subject to ornamentation. Hearts and cupids, flowers, birds, insects and animals were popular motifs. These chatelaines were often fine examples of the silversmith's art. As an alternative to the girdle chain these plates were sometimes mounted on a brooch so that they could be pinned to the dress. Although chatelaines and chatelettes (as the chatelaine pins are sometimes called) are eminently collectable in their own right they are worth very much more when complete with matching accoutrements such as scent bottle, vinaigrette, stamp box, scissors, bodkin, button hook, pen or pencil, needlecase and mirror. The number of objects usually ranged from three to six, though a few have been noted with up to ten or twelve attachments. If the chatelaine and its appendages are silver, be sure to check that the hallmarks correspond.

Chip boxes

The name is misleading, since these attractive little boxes were intended for ribbons, handkerchiefs, trinkets or sweetmeats. They were flat ovals, their sides made out of strips of plywood in the manner of modern date-boxes The sides and lid were gaudily decorated with floral patterns, or pictures of scenery, fairy tales, biblical or historic events. Others had engravings or chromolithographs pasted on the lid. Chip boxes were a speciality of the Black Forest district of Germany, but they may also be found in parts of Austria and France.

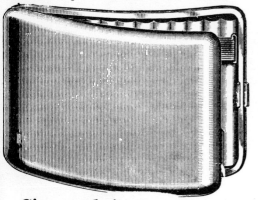

Cigar and cigarette cases

Slim cases for carrying cigars first became popular at the beginning of the nineteenth century, coinciding with the spread of cigar smoking in America and Europe. The cigars of that period were smaller and slimmer than those smoked today and could be carried in small cases quite easily. The earliest cases were made of leather or papier mâché, often richly decorated with floral motifs or geometric patterns. The early cases are comparatively rare, but after 1867, when the production of cigarettes began on a commercial basis, cases became more plentiful and, at the same time, were more varied in design and composition. Leather continued to be the most popular material, often attractively mounted with silver rims, clasps and hinges, down to the end of the last century. Metal cases came into general use in the early 1900s and rapidly developed into a major art form, rivalling the snuff box of earlier generations. Cigarette cases may be found in gold and silver, richly jewelled or enamelled, engraved or decorated with intricate repoussé work. Now that cigarette smoking is in decline, and most smokers keep their cigarettes in the pack anyway, these cases are little used, but their aesthetic and antiquarian interest is on the increase.

Cigar and tobacco cutters

The more ornamental cigar cutters should be classed as objects of vertu. Manufactured in gold or silver-gilt and sometimes set with enamels and precious stones, these cutters were an elegant ornament to the gentleman's desk or table. Smaller examples were often fitted to watch-chains or were combined with pocket lighters. Cigar cutters were at one time attached to the counters in tobacconists' shops and while their use was often free to customers, in some cases a device was fitted which meant that a coin had to be inserted first. Not common in Britain or Europe, but at one time an indispensable feature of American cigar-stores was the tobacco cutter which enabled a 'chaw' of tobacco of the requisite length to be measured off. Among the best known of these counter-top cutters was the Imp, so called on account of the tiny figure perched on top of the handle. These ubiquitous cutters retailed at a dollar each in the 1890s, but today collectors are paying twenty times that sum. Tobacco cutters may be found in all manner of shapes and sizes, incorporating animal and human figures, or even in the form of guillotines!

Coal-hole covers

The coal-hole cover is rapidly becoming a thing of the past. As central heating replaces open coal fires and as the older houses in our cities give way to modern blocks of flats the coal-hole covers which dot our pavements will disappear. In districts which have been redeveloped in recent years, literally thousands of these circular iron lids must have been discarded and most of them will have been consigned to scrap heaps and melted down. A few of them, however, have been rescued by enterprising collectors of Victoriana and as long ago as 1962 there was an exhibition devoted to them in London. Cast your eye down as you walk along the street, preferably in older districts with terraced houses, and note the immense variety of coal-hole covers. The great majority of them are circular and are made of cast iron. Often the name of the manufacturer, his address, trademark and patent number will be found inscribed round the edge – valuable source material for the industrial archaeologist of the future. They are surprisingly attractive, with geometric patterns and floral motifs predominating. It has recently become fashionable to take rubbings of coal-hole covers (using the same technique as that for taking brass rubbings from churches) and these, when mounted and framed, make unusual wall decorations.

Coal scuttles

As central heating becomes more popular the days of the coal scuttle are numbered. Now is the time to buy fine examples at bargain prices. Even if they are no longer needed for coal, they can easily be converted into containers for indoor gardens. They come in all shapes and sizes – tall hoppers and round squat bowl types, in bronze, brass and lacquered tin ware. A nineteenth century refinement was the closed scuttle or purdonium (q.v.).

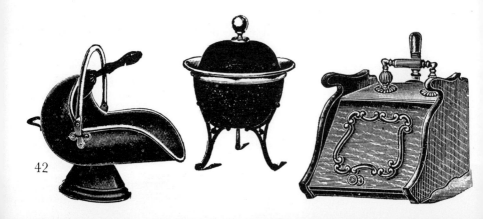

Coat hangers

There is a world of difference between the utilitarian hangers of today, made of wire, plastic or wood, and the elegant bronze or silver hangers of a century ago. These hangers were usually suspended by a chain and consisted of comparatively broad metal plates, highly ornamented with scrollwork and neo-rococo designs. Some bore intricate floral patterns while a few were embellished with human figures – angels, cherubs or mythological characters. Carved wooden hangers were also used in the nineteenth century and were suitably decorated or painted. Various patent devices for holding clothes securely were invented about this time, fitted with springs and rods for keeping the creases in trousers. Later wooden hangers in more functional form were inscribed with the names of laundries, tailoring establishments or hotels and quite an interesting collection can be made of commercial coat hangers.

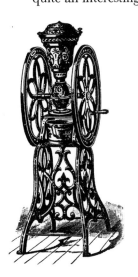

Coffee mills and grinders

These come in all shapes and sizes and, of course, are still very much in evidence – although there is a great deal of difference between the old-fashioned grinders and the streamlined modern coffee mill, operated electrically and produced in strong white plastic to blend in with the somewhat clinical surroundings of the modern kitchen. The table-top coffee mills of the last century were often elaborately decorated, with wrought or cast iron ornament on the body and legs and often surmounted by a dome shaped in some whimsical fashion. The most attractive coffee-mills were the small ones designed for use in the home. Interest is growing, however, in the large coffee grinders which were used by grocers. Examples of these large machines may sometimes be seen in the windows of coffee shops to this day. Although some of them were capable of grinding about three pounds a minute by hand, those manufactured at the turn of the century were already adapted to electric power. They were more utilitarian than the domestic mills, but were seldom bereft of some decoration at least. Their brightly polished brass and copperwork gave them a handsome appearance. Similar devices were used to grind spices and drugs.

Colanders

Modern aluminium or plastic versions of these kitchen strainers, used for draining liquids from vegetables or fruit, are not particularly attractive. But those produced 70 or 80 years ago were more decorative and varied in appearance. They were made of copper, brass, tin-ware or enamelled ware and decoration consisted of floral patterns formed by the arrangement of the holes, or on the rim, foot-rim and handles. The same decorative treatment was applied to other kitchen sieves, strainers, graters, riddles and funnels, and matching sets are worth looking out for.

Combs

The comb is defined by the *Encyclopaedia Britannica* as "a toothed toilet implement used for cleaning and arranging the hair". Combs are of great antiquity and examples in wood, bone or horn have been excavated from prehistoric sites. The Greeks and Romans favoured boxwood, while ivory was popular with the Egyptians and the Chinese used tortoiseshell. Horn and tortoiseshell were the most common materials used in the manufacture of combs in Europe and America, but these have been supplanted in recent years by plastics. In the late nineteenth century tortoiseshell combs with intricate carving and metal inlays were fashionable and fine examples of these are highly desirable today. Around the same period, however, small combs for grooming the moustache were popular with gentlemen. These were often mounted with silver and folded inside a metal case so that they could easily be carried in the pocket.

Communion tokens

In the Protestant Church, particularly in the Scottish Presbyterian form and occasionally in the French and Dutch Calvinist form, the sacrament of Communion was preceded by a service of catechism when the members of the congregation would be subject to examination on moral and spiritual matters and tested in their knowledge of the scriptures. This service took place on the Thursday before Communion and those who were regarded as fit to attend the Sunday service were given tokens which were subsequently used to gain admittance. They would be handed over to the Kirk elder on duty at the door on the morning of the Communion. The earliest Communion tokens, dating in some cases from before the Reformation of 1560, were of card (as they are nowadays) but by the beginning of the seventeenth century lead tokens were adopted. These were either cast in a simple mould or stamped out of thin lead sheets. The earliest examples are very crude, rectangular in format and uniface, with often no more than the name (or an abbreviation) of the parish. Eighteenth and nineteenth century tokens were more ambitious with biblical quotations and the date of the service. Eventually they even included coats of arms or pictorial representations of the church concerned, or Christian symbols. They were often struck in pewter but occasionally in brass or bronze.

Companion sets

Small metal stands containing poker, shovel, tongs and brush were ubiquitous in the days when everyone had coal fires. With the increase of central heating the need for companion sets has greatly diminished. At present, therefore, they are fairly plentiful – and reasonably cheap since there is, as yet, little demand for them from collectors. Both the stands and the individual fire irons were capable of decoration, and consequently a wide range of types will be found. Wrought iron, steel and brass were the materials most commonly used, though heavy bronze was fashionable for a short time in the 1880s.

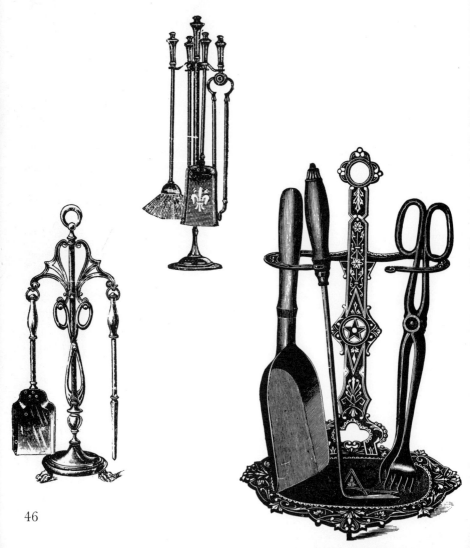

Cork pictures

The outer bark of the evergreen oak (*quercus suber*) provides the raw material for this art form. Since this tree is a native of North Africa, the Iberian peninsula and the Mediterranean countries, it is there that the art of carving intricate compositions in cork is mainly practised. A similar pastime has long been popular in India and the Far East, especially in Japan where the Abemaki tree produces a similar substance. Thin strips of the dried bark are carved in minute detail and then assembled in layers, to create a three dimensional effect. Mounted and glazed, these pictures, usually of landscapes, were once a popular feature in the bazaars of North Africa and the orient and many of them must have found their way to Northern Europe and America. On account of the brittle nature of the material, however, cork pictures are now seldom met with.

Corkscrews

The simplest type of corkscrew, a plain steel spiral with a wooden handle, has not altered in the past century. There is, however, a wealth of variety in the more elaborate types. From the beginning of this century date the combination corkscrews which incorporated bottle-openers, wire cutters and penknife. The luxury versions of the corkscrew took many forms, with handles in silver, ivory, mother-of-pearl or horn. Others had a novelty handle with miniature figures of sportsmen, horses' heads and even golf balls. Appropriately, a popular subject was the bottle itself, miniatures in silver or solid glass being mounted on the handles. Novelty corkscrews are still being manufactured, but the more desirable ones are those made before 1920.

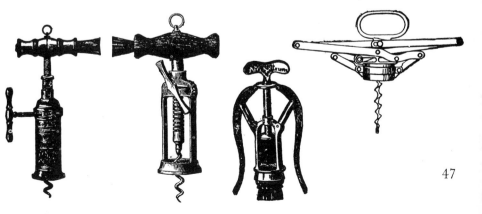

47

Costumes and accessories

Old clothing is now a respectable antique and there have been regular sales at Christie's and Sotheby's in recent years. Very few garments have survived from the seventeenth and eighteenth centuries in pristine condition; materials were expensive and therefore clothes were handed down from one generation to the next and frequently recut in accordance with current fashions. The nineteenth and early twentieth centuries offer far more scope to the collector and the literature on costume is extensive. The chronology of the introduction of various fabrics – muslin, printed cottons, challis, chintz, gingham, cashmere and merino for everyday wear and the various types of silks, satins, organdie and gauzes for evening wear – can have an important bearing on the authenticity of a garment. The introduction of materials which form a minor detail in costume is also relevant in dating an item. In 1830, for example, rubber first appeared in corsetry and elastic, while in the same year flattened copper was introduced for hooks and eyes. A decade later hooks and eyes were being made of brass wire. In 1841 alpaca was first utilised in clothing accessories and the three-fold linen button made its début. In 1843 pins were first manufactured with solid heads while the earliest safety pins came into use in 1878. Techniques of cutting and stitching can also be used to date costume. The chain-stitch sewing machine was introduced in 1856, while the earliest lock-stitch machine appeared four years later. The first aniline dies, appropriately named Magenta and Solferino after the two great battles of the Italian War of Liberation, came into use in the 1860s.

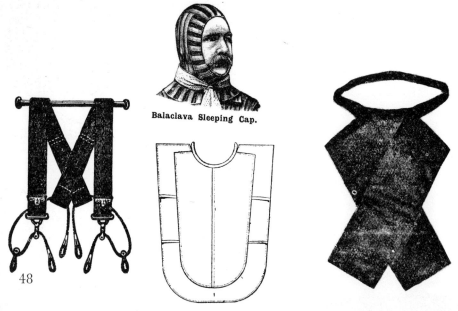

Balaclava Sleeping Cap.

48

Crumb trays and brushes

Small trays, rather like ornamental dust-pans, with matching brushes, were popular in the early decades of this century for brushing crumbs from the tablecloth after a meal. Indeed, quite a number of them are probably still in use for this purpose though their manufacture has gone into decline. Perhaps the increasing use of place mats instead of table-cloths has had something to do with this. The finest examples of these crumb tray and brush sets were manufactured in silver, and these are now relatively scarce since many of them have long since been melted down for their scrap value. For the less well-endowed, however, there was a wide range of silver-plated or electro-plated sets, and these have survived in large quantities. Farther down the scale were those manu-factured in brass, copper or pewter, while the more modern examples were chrome-plated steel. From the collector's viewpoint the chief interest lies in the pre-World War One examples characterised by lavish decoration. The brushes were usually curved to facilitate handling and their wooden backs were often covered or inlaid with metal fillets decorated to match the trays. Trays used in the nursery may also be found, decorated with scenes from fairy tales.

Curled paper work

Strips of paper were curled up into tight rolls of different shapes and diameters and then glued end on to the surface being decorated. When the pattern was completed the curled paper would be varnished, painted or gilded. This form of decoration was applied to boxes, trays or even small table tops. It was never practised on a large, commercial scale, but was a popular pastime with young ladies at the end of the eighteenth and early nineteenth centuries. Occasionally curled paper work may be found covered with glass panels on work-boxes, tea caddies and similar articles.

Darners

In these days of cheap nylon socks and stockings, darning is almost a lost art. Socks made from man-made fibres are so tough that they seldom spring holes – and if they do they are usually discarded. Not so long ago, however, hose were made of wool or silk and comparatively expensive. To assist in the domestic chore of darning, small round objects were inserted into the stocking to hold the afflicted area taut. In poor families a potato would do the trick admirably, but most households used something a bit more permanent. Darners, or darning eggs as they are sometimes called, were usually wooden hemispheres mounted on a handle. The majority of the wooden ones were utilitarian in design but the earlier ones are worth collecting as fine examples of hand-turning. From the collector's viewpoint, however, the main interest lies in darners made of glass, ivory, hardstone, earthenware or porcelain, the latter being decorated with pictures or floral vignettes. They were usually elliptical rather than completely round, hence the name 'egg', or had a handle fitted to them, and these handles were sometimes made of silver. Hollow darners, with compartments for thimbles and thread, were patented in the 1870s.

Dentures

False teeth have a surprisingly long history in one form or another. Etruscan goldsmiths, a thousand years before the Christian era, were practising cosmetic dentistry and had evolved ingenious types of bridge-work. Dentures, either partial or complete, came into use in the late seventeenth century. Prior to about 1850 dentures were held in position by means of spiral springs. Early dentures were fearsome devices. Teeth stripped from corpses on the field of battle were set into a base carved from ivory, bone or wood. Those who could afford it steeped their dentures in port wine overnight in order to make them more palatable, but there can be no doubt that antique dentures were singularly unpleasant. Rembrandt Peale's portrait makes it clear that George Washington was a martyr to ill-fitting teeth. Had he lived a little longer he might have benefited from the improved dentures invented in America about 1800. Springs were replaced by a base plate which extended over the hard palate. Early in the nineteenth century wax and plaster were used to take impressions and dentures were then made of porcelain. Vulcanite was introduced about 1860 and remained in use until about 1935. All-metal dentures were common in Europe. It should not be difficult to acquire a wide-ranging, if slightly macabre, collection of these aids.

Distaffs

These are devices which were employed in rudimentary forms of spinning by hand. They consisted of short sticks, known in America as 'rocks', round one end of which the flax or wool was loosely wound and from which it was spun off by the spindle. Because hand-spinning was traditionally regarded as women's work, the 'distaff' side of the family refers to the female branch, as opposed to the 'spear' or male branch. January 7th, the day after Epiphany when the twelve days of the Christmas holiday came to an end, was popularly known as St. Distaff's Day, as women then returned to their chores. Distaffs are rather hard to find nowadays, though in parts of the Outer Hebrides you will still see women working with them. The styles range from plain turned wood to the ornately carved and painted distaffs used in Scandinavia, the Low Countries, France, Italy and Spain. The flax distaffs used in the southern states of America were complicated affairs, resembling a primitive gyroscope or spinning-top. Decorated distaffs, embellished with metal bosses or straw-plaiting, may be found in parts of Europe. They were sometimes given as love tokens and often bear lovers' knots, hearts, cupids and other appropriate symbols.

Door-bells

Apart from the bells or chimes themselves (which come in a great assortment of shapes and types) considerable interest lies in the circular plates and bell-pulls which were affixed to the door-post. These may be found in bronze and brass and, less commonly, in iron. Often a great deal of ornament and ingenuity was lavished on the circular plates, with geometric or floral patterns. Rotary door-bells were fashionable from about 1880 onwards and many of them are in use to this day. In this case the bell was rung by turning a small metal key. Other bells were activated by means of levers or slide-pulls. Yet another type of bell, which offers tremendous scope to the collector, is that used inside the house and connected with the servants' quarters. These bells were operated by handles attached to the wall (usually at the side of the fireplace). In keeping with the boudoirs and drawing-rooms which they adorned, these handles were often highly ornate and may be found in porcelain, ebony and ivory as well as wood and various metals. Gilding and inlay-work on wood or metal handles, and underglaze decoration on the ceramic examples, extended the variety of these items. Many attractive bells have come to light on account of the demolition of older houses in recent years.

C.F.G.&CO.

Drawer handles and knobs

A great deal of late nineteenth and early twentieth century furniture was undistinguished and has not been considered worth preserving. It has been dismantled or, at worst, chopped up for firewood. The only residue of such furniture is the hardware which garnished it. As a result most junkyards accumulate surprising quantities of drawer pulls, handles and knobs which, being infinitely more durable than the furniture they originally graced, can be used time and time again on other pieces. However, many of these items are worth collecting for their own sakes, suitably mounted on boards for display. It is surprising how many different types of metal fitment have been used on drawers – pulls, handles, knobs and rings and each in great variety. Drawer handles and pulls in fancy designs were popular (though not always practical) in late Victorian times, shaped like animal masks or vine-leaves with lots of tendrils and awkward edges. Drop handles and knobs were often made of glass or porcelain as well as metal, and likewise offer enormous scope to the collector.

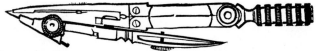

Drawing instruments

Instruments for accurate technical drawing are as old as Euclid and Pythagoras, but the majority of extant examples date from the late Middle Ages when the Renaissance gave tremendous impetus to the study of geometry and draughtsmanship. From the sixteenth century onwards instruments giving a high degree of accuracy were produced to meet the growing demands of scientists, astronomers and engineers. Rules, T-squares, triangles and semi-circles were usually made from brass. Care was lavished on the calibration of measurements and angles and the surfaces of these instruments were often decorated with fine engraving; including the name of the instrument maker and sometimes the date of manufacture. The more sumptuous examples were inlaid with silver, or were made entirely of silver, though the softness of this metal rendered it unsatisfactory for everyday draughtsmanship. Other metals such as bronze and tinplate were and are used, while bone, wood and ivory were the most popular non-metallic substances. Compasses and dividers are also collectable, though usually less decorative. Complete sets of drawing instruments dating before 1850 are rare and now fetch high prices, but later sets, in polished wooden cases, are more frequently met with and worth looking out for.

Electrical apparatus

With the words 'Mr. Watson, come here, I want you', the modern age of electricity began. On March 10th, 1876, Alexander Graham Bell transmitted this sentence to his assistant over the first telephone. By the mid-1880s the telephone was an increasingly common feature in both homes and offices. Early hand-sets, in lacquered and gilded metal, are highly popular nowadays, not so much for their proper use but for conversion into lamps or table lighters. Electric lamps were invented by Edison and J. W. Swan independently, between 1878 and 1880. There cannot be many examples of early carbon lamp bulbs in existence today. Subsequent types – the osmium lamp (1898), the tantalum lamp (1903) and the modern tungsten lamp (1904) – are more plentiful. Electric lamps themselves offer plenty of material to the collector, ranging from the most functional desk-lights to the highly ornamental bronze lamps sculpted in the shape of the American *danseuse* Loie Fuller. Electric cigar lighters were in use by 1890 and electric radiators by 1900. Other electric gadgets worth considering include early radio and television sets, gramophones (phonographs), electric motors, fans and telegraphic equipment.

Electric Copper Kettle.

Electric Shaving Pot.
100 or 200 volt.

Enamelled coins

In Victorian times it was fashionable to make jewellery out of coins by applying enamel to different parts of their surface. Enamelled coins were mounted on watch-chains, bracelets, cuff-links, ear-rings and brooches when the Jubilee series appeared in 1887. The best enamelling was carried out in Birmingham by W. H. Probert and Edwin Steele during the last two decades of the nineteenth century. Coin-enamelling survived on the continent of Europe as late as 1920 where the French jeweller Louis Elic Millenet specialised in this art. The coins most often treated in this way were the crowns showing St. George and the Dragon, the Jubilee series already mentioned bearing the royal coat of arms, the Peacock rupees of Burma and the early five-franc pieces from France. Fine examples of enamelled coins can be picked up in jewellers' shops and curio shops.

Envelope and stamp moisteners

These office accessories, which are still very much in use, first appeared in the 1840s following the introduction of adhesive postage stamps. The early British stamps had the following instruction in the sheet margin 'In Wetting the Back be careful not to remove the Cement'. Doubts as to the composition of the 'cement' (which was only potato starch) made people wary of licking their stamps – and this encouraged the manufacture of the various gadgets. They ranged from small circular cups containing pieces of sponge, to large metal, glass or ceramic containers which held a roller revolving in a trough. A refinement of this form was a roller with a gummed surface; this type was (and is) more suitable for gumming wrapping paper. Some of the more elaborate envelope moisteners also incorporated ink wells, pen-rests and side compartments for stamps. Nowadays, of course, plastics form the basis for most envelope moisteners, but seventy years ago brass, silver, porcelain and pressed or cut-glass were popularly used and a wide variety of styles of decoration was employed.

Erasers

There is nothing permanent – far less collectable – about the modern eraser, which consists solely of a small bar or block of india-rubber. A century ago, however, erasers were much more substantial affairs, mounted in a holder of brass, ivory or even silver, to match the other accessories in a writing set or ink stand (qq.v.). Silver-mounted erasers, in particular, were often intricately decorated, and tend to have survived rather better than their base metal counterparts. Late Victorian school erasers were mounted on enamelled tinplate, sometimes embellished with characters from nursery rhymes or fairy tales. Examples of these in good condition are understandably scarce.

Feather pictures

Pictures of birds composed of actual feathers were a late eighteenth century speciality of certain British artists. The arrangement of the feathers in a montage may be regarded as a cross between taxidermy and representational art, since the feathers of the bird depicted were used as far as possible, and glass beads were sometimes added to simulate the eyes, but other appendages such as the beak and feet were merely painted in. Usually the bird was depicted as in life, but the more bizarre pictures showed the bird as a 'still life', to put it euphemistically. Some of these feather pictures, in fact, look like something run over by a steam-roller, and the presence of a gout of bright red blood trickling from the subject merely heightens the illusion !

Fire insurance marks

The observant eye will often note, high on the walls of old buildings in London and other cities of Britain, symbols and badges. These are the emblems of the fire insurance companies who were responsible, at one time, for fire prevention and extinction. The Royal Exchange was the first of these companies to possess fire engines, this step being taken in 1722. Many other companies soon followed and this gave rise to the practice of placing marks on the buildings they insured so that each fire brigade would give special attention to any premises insured with their own company. The various insurance companies combined their fire-fighting resources in 1833 and responsibility was taken over by the Metropolitan Board of Works in 1865. The fire marks found on buildings thus belong to the period from 1722 to 1833 or slightly later. Redevelopment in the cities of London and Westminster, Birmingham, Manchester, Liverpool and Bristol has yielded large numbers of these attractive old metal plaques and stimulated the interest of collectors in recent years.

Flat-irons

Even the electric iron has less use than before in this day and age of drip-dry, non-iron fabrics, but it is not so long ago that ironing was one of the major household chores. Up to World War Two non-electric flat-irons were the rule rather than the exception. The simplest were solid metal in construction and were heated before an open fire. A later refinement was the box iron which had a receptacle for red-hot coals which maintained the heat of the iron at a more even temperature. Charcoal irons, as their name suggests, contained an ingenious charcoal 'oven'. Direrent sizes and shapes of iron were produced for different purposes, from bed sheets to lace collars. Decoration could be, and often was, lavished on the wooden handles and their metal supports, while the matching iron-stands, usually of fretted iron or brass, were often ornamented with intricate openwork patterns. Flat-irons and stands are still quite plentiful, having found a subsidiary purpose in farms and country houses as door stops, but more and more of them are being gathered into antique shops.

Food mixers, beaters and grinders

Gadgets used in the preparation of food are legion nowadays, but it is only within the past century that they have become commonplace. The early examples in tin-ware, cast-iron, brass or copper with wooden handles and bases, have an attractive other-worldly appearance and make interesting ornaments when highly polished. Among the old-time kitchen gadgets may be mentioned fruit and vegetable slicers, cole slaw cutters, meat mincers, batter whisks, graters, apple parers, grist mills and fruit presses. Often a lick of paint will transform an otherwise mundane article into a decorative object.

Foot warmers

These are portable stoves or receptacles for hot coals which served to warm the feet in cold weather. They resemble low stools, and one can just imagine the luxury at the end of a day exposed to rain or trudging through slush and snow when one could pull off one's boots and put one's feet up on one of these foot warmers. These home comforts were popular in northern and eastern Europe until about 1900, or even later in remote areas. Those from Scandinavia, Russia, Poland and Switzerland were usually of wood, intricately carved or painted and fretted in order to let the warm air circulate freely. Inside would be a small metal charcoal burner or container for coals. In Austria, France, Germany and Northern Italy, foot warmers were more commonly made in metals such as wrought iron, copper or brass. Occasionally earthenware was used. Similar warmers were also used in carriages for the same purpose. Miniature versions were produced for ladies who carried them in their muffs to warm their hands. Warming-pans were a distinct variant of the foot warmer, specially adapted for warming and airing beds.

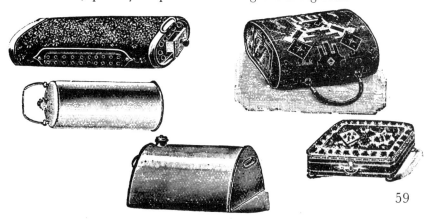

Fountain pens

These pens revolutionised the art of writing when they first became popular in the 1880s and rapidly ousted the ordinary steel pen. Now they, in turn, are being overtaken by the ballpoint, though it is unlikely that they will ever die out entirely. Various attempts were made in the nineteenth century to devise a pen which would not disturb the writer's train of thought by needing to be dipped regularly in an ink-well. It was not until the 1880s, however, that a suitable feed device had been evolved, so that the flow of ink from the reservoir to the nib could be regulated. Early fountain pens suffered terribly from a distressing tendency to leak unless carried upright. Early this century various safety types were devised, in which spiral grooves with a gravity rod controlled the flow of ink to the nib and effectively sealed it when not in use. The cap of the pen usually contains a plug which completes this sealing process. Thousands of different brands of pen have been manufactured in the past ninety years and examples can be picked up at relatively little expense. They present a surprising variety in shape, style and technical structure.

Fruit bowls and baskets

Few homes, even now, are without a bowl of fruit sitting on a sideboard, and the decorative fruit bowl is still one of the great wedding present stand-bys. The range is truly enormous. At one end there are handsome bowls in turned woodware relying on a high polish for aesthetic appeal. At the other end are the silver fruit bowls and baskets which were so popular at one time for presentation purposes, usually to employees for long and faithful service. In between comes the range of bowls in pressed or moulded glass with mounts in silver-plate or chrome. The glass bowls were a speciality of the American glass manufacturing houses and demonstrated the versatility of their products around the turn of the century. Many a fine example of mother-of-pearl glass, amberina, peach-blow or kew blas – to name only a few – may be found in this relatively neglected medium. Pottery and porcelain are also used for fruit bowls, though these tend to be less decorative and therefore less collectable.

Frying pans

Not, at first glance, likely to be a collectable item – and yet a range of different-sized copper frying pans make an attractive wall decoration for the kitchen. Ignoring the strictly utilitarian steel or non-stick pans of the present day there are plenty of different types which are worth collecting. Apart from the copper pans there are tinware frying pans with long, elegant wooden handles which were popular a century ago, or frying pans in a combination of iron, brass or bronze. The handles of these old-fashioned utensils were often surprisingly ornamental considering their utilitarian purpose.

Gambling equipment

Biblical references to 'casting lots', dice-throwing and other forms of gambling indicate the great antiquity of this human weakness. It seems to be world-wide in its application and over the centuries has taken many different forms. Some adjuncts of gambling have long been collected in their own right; playing cards dating from the Middle Ages are a good example. Other kinds of gambling equipment, however, are worth considering as collectable objects. Dice, for example, have evolved, over a period of time covering roughly 2000 years, from the primitive 'bones' used by Roman soldiers to the ivory pieces used today. An interesting field, as yet little explored, is that covering the devices and equipment of gambling – score boards and cards used in cribbage, dominoes, roulette wheels and early mechanical devices which were the ancestors of the modern one-armed bandits. And do not overlook the collecting possibilities of gaming tokens and counters, ranging from the fake brass spade guineas of the eighteenth century and the 'jacks' of the nineteenth, to the handsome nickel and franklinium dollar-sized tokens used in the casinos and gaming-clubs of the present day.

Games and puzzles

Considering the wear and tear they must have endured at the hands of youthful users, it is surprising that the games and puzzles of a hundred and more years ago have survived at all. But a search through attics and lumber-rooms has brought to light a wide range of such items, for which there is now a growing market. The popularity of Victorian and Edwardian games is due largely to a spirit of nostalgia, though an increasing number of collectors were not even born when these games were at the height of their popularity. Vintage sets of such old favourites as halma, l'attaque, moneta and logos (the forerunner of scrabble) are now eagerly sought. Less intellectual games such as bagatelle, parlour quoits, tiddlywinks and ludo have their modern counterparts, but it is the early versions of these pastimes which are most desirable. Card games were used extensively in the nineteenth century for quasi-educational purposes. Yesterday's equivalents of Happy Families included Celebrated Poets, Hidden Book Titles, Peerless Authors and others designed to teach literature, history and geography painlessly. The early jig-saw puzzles also had a strongly didactic approach, the completed picture being in some way instructional.

FISH POND GAME.

"THE TANDEM PARTY."

Or Putting Girl on Bicycle

Cut out the female figures and number them on the back. Attach the sheet with the tandem to a convenient place on the wall or to the door. Blindfold the players, who advance in succession from a distance of seven feet towards the sheet, and where they touch it first with one arm fully outstretched, there they pin the lady figure on the sheet. The winner is the one who pins the figure nearest to the front seat.

Printed on cloth. The size of the sheet is 36x36,

LOGOS.

A GAME OF WORDS
(NEW)

Garters

The garter is almost a thing of the past. But it will probably always have some significance as an erotic symbol and therefore continue to be highly decorative. Even when the garter was necessary as a means of holding up ladies' stockings it was usually ornamental, leading one to suppose that, even in Victorian times, it was meant to be seen. The silk, satin and elastic webbing of nineteenth century garters may not have survived too well, but the metal buckles are more durable and are quite collectable in their own right. These metal buckles were invariably decorated or formed in fancy designs. Gold or silver buckles, of course, are very expensive, but the trinket trays in jewellers' shops will often yield interesting examples in plated bronze or brass with enamel or jewelled decoration. Buckles in the form of the heads of animals, seashells, hearts or cupid's bows were perennial favourites. 'Novelty' buckles of a more risqué type were popular in the Naughty Nineties and are now keenly sought.

Gasmasks

The time between the first chlorine attack at Ypres in 1915 and the threat of chemical and biological warfare at the present day is relatively short, but though, thankfully, gas has seldom been used as a weapon since World War One, except in riot control, the devices offering protection against it have advanced enormously. As the gases used in World War One became deadlier the respirators used became more and more sophisticated. The first masks were simply gauze pads soaked in phenol. By the end of the war, however, gasmasks offering complete protection to eyes and lungs had been developed. It is surprising how varied these masks were. Rubberised cloth was used by the British, Americans and French, oiled leather by the Germans, cast-iron by the Italians. The gasmasks used by the Russians completely enveloped the head and must have been extremely uncomfortable. Preventing the eye-pieces from misting up was a major problem, and various ingenious devices such as nose-clips and mouth-tubes, impregnated glass and air intake systems were invented. The gasmasks of World War One are now collected as a separate branch of militaria or as part of the equipment of a particular army or period. Not so long ago they could be picked up at give-away prices but now rare or unusual types may cost anything up to £20. They occasionally turn up in army surplus stores, but antique shops specialising in arms, armour and militaria are the main source nowadays.

Gipsy wagons

Now that most gipsies, tinkers and other travellers use motorised caravans and trailers the old painted wooden wagon is virtually a thing of the past. Not so long ago groups of these wagons were colourful sights in lay-bys and on roadsides in rural Britain. Fortunately many of them have been preserved in all their gaudy glory by collectors nostalgic for the era before the coming of the motor car. Gipsy wagons are now the 'in' thing as children's adventure play rooms. In this age of the two-car family the possession of a gipsy wagon has become a status symbol. Several distinct types of wagon were being made in Britain up to the outbreak of World War Two, with picturesque names like Barrel-topped, Showman, Bow-topped, Yorkshire Bell and Cottage Wagon, differing in size, lay-out, shape of roof and type of shafts. Similar wagons were manufactured all over Europe at one time. Incidentally, though generally more prosaic in appearance, wooden farm carts are also finding a market these days. They vary in size from small hand carts to large hay wagons. Brightly painted, they are now being used as garden ornaments and stands for plants and flower pots.

Hafner ware

A type of lead-glazed pottery, popular in Germany from the late Middle Ages to the seventeenth century, it takes its name from the German word *Hafner*, meaning a stove-maker. The earliest application of this type of pottery was to the tiles which decorated the great German stoves of the period. The potteries of Nuremberg in Bavaria, and the Baltic port of Lübeck, specialised in hafner ware. As well as the distinctive green-glazed tiles with raised decoration, these potteries produced jugs, vases and dishes in various shades of green, blue, brown or purple. The decoration varied enormously, though Biblical and historical figures and heraldic subjects were popular. Hafner ware was superseded in the seventeenth century by tin-glazed enamelled wares, variously known as maiolica, fayence or delft. Examples of true hafner ware are now scarce and mainly confined to museum collections.

Hair ornaments

Hat-pins are mentioned separately, but there are many other collectable objects connected with lady's coiffeurs. When hair-styles were infinitely more elaborate than they are today a great many pins and combs were required to keep the hair and the hair-pieces in place. Before the advent of the modern kirby grip, hair pins were often large and highly decorative affairs in silver set with jewels or enamel inlay. The back and side combs were also made of silver, or even gold, and richly decorated with precious or semi-precious stones. Less elaborate (and more plentiful) are those made of tortoiseshell, ivory, mother-of-pearl or horn. They were often intricately carved or engraved and also set with jewels. Many of these combs had ornaments in the shape of birds, flowers and butterflies mounted at the top. Other hair ornaments were called *barrettes* – slides or clasps for holding the strands of hair in position. These were likewise decorated according to contemporary fashion. Less elaborate, but still quite collectable, are the jewelled bandeaux and hair-ribbons which were popular in the 1920s and 1930s. Hair jewellery is a vast subject, and one which has received relatively little attention until now.

Hand-cuffs and leg-irons

Restraining devices may seem rather an odd thing to collect, but they apparently have a large following. For some curious reason they are regarded as a facet of militaria and can often be picked up in antique shops specialising in arms and armour. The commonest are the hand-cuffs, of which many different kinds have been used by police and law enforcement officers in the past hundred and fifty years. In addition there are chain devices, known as 'twisters', for securing the captive's wrists. Less common are leg-irons, complete with ball and chain, and iron wrist bands also fitted with heavy iron balls, which served the purpose of restricting the prisoner's movements. Fortunately such instruments are now a thing of the past.

Hat pins

In the days when women wore elaborate hair-dos and large hats, the hat pin was a very necessary item of dress. Great ingenuity was lavished on the shape, composition and decoration of the head of these pins. From the plain silver pins with geometric designs popular in the Art Deco style of the twenties to the fancy jewelled examples from the 1880s the range of ornamentation involved is virtually unlimited. Among the novelty shapes found on hat pins may be mentioned crowns, flowers, human heads, animals, birds and musical instruments. Pins were ornamented with pearls and precious stones or paste jewellery, porcelain or various metals. Hat pins can be mounted on lengths of cloth for display purposes, but it is a better idea to get hold of an antique hat pin holder, which is an appropriate way of showing off such a collection. These holders, manufactured a century ago right up to Edwardian times, may be found in wood, ivory, glass, porcelain or metal, and were themselves often highly decorative and collectable.

Hooks

Hooks for hanging things on come in a multitude of shapes and sizes. The commonest type is the clothes-hook, which came into general use in the 1850s and is still indispensable. Such hooks were usually made of iron (often lacquered or given a bronze finish) or brass, but this belies the diversity of shape and decoration of which they were capable, ranging from delicately wrought iron-work to the elegant hooks with porcelain ornament and gilding intended for ladies' boudoirs. Particularly desirable are hooks of 1890 to 1910 with elaborate Art Nouveau decoration, sometimes incorporating flowers and human figures. Hooks were usually made with single or double prongs, though unusual types with as many as five prongs have been noted. They may be found with open-work decoration or in bronze inlaid with brass, or even enamelled in contrasting colours. Some very complicated coat and hat hooks in the early years of this century included small mirrors. Hooks for suspending bird cages are of greater antiquity than clothes hooks and highly desirable examples from the eighteenth century may be found with rococo decoration. Other collectable varieties include lamp-hooks and pot-hooks, though these were usually less ornate than the others. Picture hooks may be found with elaborate moulding and die stamping.

Hot water bottles

The warming pan was gradually superseded in the mid-nineteenth century by the hot water bottle which, in turn, was finally supplanted by the rubber hot water bag (still known as a bottle) after World War Two. There was a considerable overlap between the various types. The rubber hot water bottle was already in use in the closing years of the last century, while the earthenware 'pig' was still being sold in rural hardware and general stores until about twenty years ago. The stone or earthenware pigs were cylindrical, flattened on one side to prevent them from rolling around the bed. For added comfort they were provided with flannel covers which were often decorated with embroidery. Earlier than the earthenware pig, hot water bottles were made of brass, tinware or copper and were circular in shape with a screw stopper at one side. These metal bottles, brightly polished, make attractive ornaments. Like the pigs, they were usually covered to protect the toes from burning. The embroidery of the covers was yet another way in which Victorian and Edwardian ladies whiled away the time and indulged their passion for decorating even the most mundane objects.

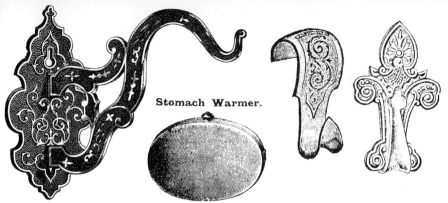
Stomach Warmer.

Ice picks and awls

Long before the advent of the electric refrigerator, ice was commonly used for freezing and chilling food. Implements for cutting and chipping ice are therefore of great antiquity. Many different types of instrument were used a century ago for this purpose. Ice picks, for example, could be simple steel spikes set in a wooden handle, or intricate objects with spring action handles. Collectors distinguish between the late nineteenth century factory-produced picks and the earlier examples with hand-forged blades, the latter being keenly sought after. Awls for cutting blocks of ice had fairly thick blades and pointed picks attached to iron or wooden handles. More elaborate implements included ice shavers, chisels and chippers. Machine ice-breakers were patented at the beginning of this century, equipped with rotating steel combs which controlled the fineness or coarseness of the ice chips required.

Infant feeding bottles

Nursery articles offer tremendous scope to the collector and some have been mentioned earlier in this book. One would not have thought that feeding bottles had much to offer, but in fact the Victorian examples come in a wide variety of shapes, sizes and materials – far more varied than their modern counterparts. Many were whimsical in shape, with animals and fairy-tale characters moulded or pressed into the glass. When the infant was weaned, and moved on to solid foods, there were pap boats – a revolting name which almost conjures up the mess into which the baby undoubtedly got himself at meal-times! Pap boats in earthenware or porcelain were also decorated with nursery characters and are worth looking for if they can be found in reasonable condition. Unfortunately, one imagines that the rate of breakage was high, since such items are elusive nowadays.

See also Alphabet Plates and Baby Rattles.

Ink pots

Ink as a substance for writing is almost as old as the art of writing itself and, till comparatively recently, it was little changed in composition. The oldest kind of ink consisted of carbon (usually lampblack) suspended in water, and its use has been recorded from medieval Europe to China and Japan. Lampblack mixed with gum was made into cakes which were dissolved in water as and when required. Ink in a permanent liquid form was usually a solution of ferrous sulphate and tannin from nut-galls. Ink pots are of great antiquity, having been recorded from China in the pre-Christian era, but their use in Europe was virtually confined to monasteries until the thirteenth century. From then onwards their rise gradually spread, reaching its peak in the late nineteenth century. Ink pots were made of horn, pewter, earthenware or brass and early examples have a certain primitive charm. Highly ornate ink pots became fashionable in the late nineteenth century, often as part of ink-stands or writing sets (qq.v.), but with the spread of ball point pens since World War Two they have all but disappeared from general use.

Ink stands

Stands for containing ink wells, pens and other writing materials became popular about 1840, although examples have been recorded from the late seventeenth century onwards. Higher standards of literacy and im-proved postal facilities encouraged the popularity of letter writing in the mid-nineteenth century. This coincided with the rising demand of the new middle classes for all manner of decorative articles for their homes. Thus ink stands in great profusion and countless varieties were produced for the desk and writing table. The majority of ink stands consisted of a square pot containing ink, with an elaborately mounted stopper and a metal stand which was similarly ornamented. Stands may be encountered with tiny drawers beneath the ink pot for sealing-wafers or postage stamps. More complicated ink stands would have two ink pots (one for black or blue ink, the other for red) and perhaps incor-porate an envelope moistener and pin cup. The most interesting ink stands are those made out of rams' or deer heads, horses' hooves or buffalo horns, suitably mounted with silver. Ink stands were produced in brass, silver, iron, porcelain, glass, pottery and even papier mâché. Those in malachite or lapis lazuli, with gold mounts, which were a speciality of Russian court jewellers eighty years ago, are priced beyond the range of most collectors.

Juice extractors

Before the era of the electric mixer various kinds of manual juice extractors or fruit pressers were in common use. The simplest were earthenware, iron or wooden squeezers in which pressure was applied by means of a lever to crush fruit in a chamber, the fruit juice running out through holes in the bottom of the chamber. More elaborate types had screw presses operated by means of a crank handle. Fruit presses dating from the eighteenth century form an interesting branch of woodware.

Keys

Most households accumulate large collections of keys at some time or another. Even when the locks which originally fitted the keys have long since been abandoned keys are often retained in the fond hope that perhaps they may come in handy some day. They seldom, if ever, do, but we continue to hoard old keys nevertheless. Though most modern keys are strictly functional in appearance it is amazing how much variety they present, in shape, size and type. They range from tiny keys for lockets to massive door keys and include such novelties as folding keys, Bramah keys and mortice bolts. The invention of the lever tumbler lock in the eighteenth century paved the way for the keys patented in England by Jeremiah Chubb and in the United States by Linus Yale, now in universal use. The rounded, flattened heads of these keys permit considerable freedom in decoration and inscription and even the modern examples are varied in appearance. Wooden keys were used in Egypt centuries B.C. and bronze keys from Roman times until the fourteenth century. Thereafter wrought iron was extensively used. Brass and silver keys from the eighteenth and nineteenth centuries, often highly ornamented, are keenly sought after today, but even the more prosaic examples are worth looking out for.

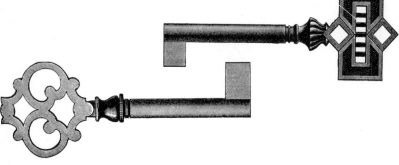

Kitchen ware

This is a vast subject which deserves a book to itself. A number of the more important groups of kitchen gadgets and utensils are the subject of separate entries in this book. A little imagination and a determined browse round junk shops and scrap yards will no doubt suggest many more.

See also Apple Scoops, Biscuit Tins, Bottle Openers, Bread Boards, Caddy Spoons, Can Openers, Cake Moulds, Casters, Coffee Mills, Colanders, Cork Screws, Food Mixers, Beaters and Grinders, Frying Pans, Ice Picks, Juice Extractors, Meat Cleavers, Meat Jacks, Mangle Boards, Mote Skimmers, Mustard Pots, Nutmeg Graters, Pickle Jars, Rack Plates, Scales and Balances, Salt and Pepper Sets, Sugar Tongs, Trays, Toasting Forks, Wooden Spoons, Wooden Measures and Waffle Irons.

Lacquer ware

This art has long been practised in China and Japan where the gum of the *Rhus vernicifera* provides the basic ingredient. Various pigments were added to this gum to produce the distinctive yellow, red and green lacquers which are now so highly prized, but shades of brown or black are those more commonly met with. True lacquering was a long and tedious process and this explains the costliness of imported Chinese or Japanese lacquer ware in the seventeenth century. European craftsmen soon devised a tolerable substitute – shellac – compounded of resin from the beetle *Coccoslacca* and alcohol. European lacquer ware was exceedingly popular in Britain, Germany and the Low Countries in the eighteenth century and fine examples are still plentiful, at a price. Though the practice of lacquering on wood declined at the end of that century it was applied increasingly to the papier mâché furniture and objects manufactured in the first half of the nineteenth century. Work boxes, writing cases and fire screens of lacquered papier mâché are now enjoying a revival in popularity.

Lamp shades

Decorative lamp shades are comparatively modern, dating from the introduction of incandescent gas light in the mid-nineteenth century. The development of electric light towards the end of the century stimulated the production of lamp shades to modify the harsh glare of this form of lighting. Lamp shades have been made of all sorts of material (including some gruesome relics of Nazi concentration camps) but those most eminently collectable were made of 'art' glass at the end of the last century. Thomas Webb in England and Louis Tiffany in the United States were the foremost exponents of the art of glass lamp shade. Fine examples of Webbs' Queen's Burmese Ware or Tiffany's famous iridescent glass are now extremely popular and therefore highly priced, but there are many kinds of art glass made by less well-known companies which are worth looking for. Moreover, while the market in vases and bowls is very keen, comparatively little interest has so far been shown in lamp shades of the same material and quality. Large quantities of shades by Steuben, Hobbs Brockunier, Mount Washington and other American glass houses were exported to Europe before World War One, but are now rapidly being repatriated – so prices are beginning to rise steadily.

Letter openers

Otherwise known as paper knives, these objects came into use in the mid-nineteenth century when envelopes became popular. Prior to that time, when letters consisted of folded sheets secured with sealing wax, opening was effected by breaking or cutting the seals with a pen-knife. Letter openers were – and still are – often miniature examples of the cutler's art at its best, with fine steel blades set into ornamental handles of ivory, mother-of-pearl or carved wood. Often they resembled miniature daggers or swords, with elaborately jewelled or inlaid handles, complete with decorated scabbards. Since a fine cutting edge is not essential to the efficiency of a letter opener, materials other than steel have been used for the blades. Brass, silver and even gold have been used for letter openers, while wood, horn and ivory are frequently met with. Victorian wooden letter openers may be found with *chinoiseries* on a black lacquered background. Particularly interesting are those decorated with landscapes and figures. Others of a more practical nature were inscribed with postal rates or tables of weights and measures.

Liberty ware

Arthur Lasenby Liberty (1843–1917), the son of a Nottingham lace manufacturer, became manager of the shop in London's Regent Street which he eventually transformed into a show piece for the Arts and Crafts Movement. He gained control of the shop (originally an Oriental emporium) in 1875 and immediately he began to adapt eastern art in weaving and design to western requirements, becoming a household word for both textiles and furnishings. He was strongly influenced by the Pre-Raphaelites and derived a great deal of inspiration from the medieval romanticism fashionable in the late nineteenth century. Wallpaper and soft furnishings in the inimitable Liberty style are comparatively hard to find nowadays, but more plentiful are the metal wares, in bronze, brass, copper and pewter which had such brand names as Cymric and Tudric (inspired by the Arthurian legends which also served as material for the Pre-Raphaelites). The range of metal wares was vast, from jewel boxes and tea caddies to cake stands and coal scuttles. The more luxurious articles were decorated with enamel inlays or semi-precious stones. It is interesting to note that what is known in English as *Art Nouveau* is known in France as *Le Stile Liberty*!

Lithophanes

Thin, flat plaques of porcelain with moulded intaglio decoration on the reverse side were popular from about 1830 to 1900 as a form of decorative panel on food warmers and lamps. For their decorative quality to be appreciated they had to be viewed against a light so that the various depths of the intaglio created a sculptured effect. They seem to have originated in Germany and marked examples have been recorded from Meissen and Berlin, though it is probable that they were also manufactured in France and England. The smallest examples were employed as panels in night lights; the largest, up to a foot square, were mounted on metal stands and used for wall lights or hand screens. They are sometimes found in the base of drinking mugs and this may have provoked the idea of simulating lithophanes in pressed glass for the same purpose. Such glass lithophanes were a speciality of the American glass houses in the late nineteenth century.

Love tokens

Occasionally one comes across coins in junk shops which turn out to be not quite what they seemed at first sight. They are coins which have been worn or polished smooth and then engraved with a date and the name of a man or woman (or both). Sometimes a motto or sentimental inscription is added which gives a clue to the purpose of the 'coin'. This practice appears to have been at its height in the eighteenth century, the commonest coins employed being the copper halfpence of George III (c. 1770–75), though Victorian coppers and foreign coins are sometimes found. Base metal coins were most favoured, but occasionally silver or even gold coins were treated in this way. The names or initials are those of two lovers and the date signifies either betrothal or marriage. Pieces have been recorded with inscriptions commemorating an anniversary, such as a silver or golden wedding. The addition of cupids, pierced hearts and other symbols of love helps the collector to recognise these love tokens at a glance. More rarely one finds elaborate engravings of lovers and courting scenes and the simple motto sometimes gives way to a lengthy inscription, running to many words, in which the lover declares his affection for his sweetheart. The style of engraving varies greatly, from crudely punched initials to the ornate and finely executed pictures done by an accomplished artist. A popular, though tedious, technique was 'pin-hole' work in which the engraving was achieved by stamping the surface of the coin with a fine-pointed punch; as many as thirty pricks might be required to form a single letter. Few of these tokens were pierced for suspension on a necklace or bracelet and from their worn condition it seems more likely that they were carried in a pocket or purse as a lucky piece.

Magic lanterns

These forerunners of the slide projector are currently enjoying renewed popularity, as are the games and puzzles of a bygone generation. Nostalgic memories of old-time party treats and concerts are evoked by these cumbersome machines. They evolved in the early nineteenth century out of ordinary lanterns designed to project a beam of light in one particular direction by the use of metal slides into which were set a converging lens with the light source at approximately the focus of the lens. From the primitive 'bullseye' developed the magic lantern whose flame could be intensified by a complicated battery of lenses and used to project an image on to a screen. The early magic lanterns were large and cumbersome and operated by candle, spirit flame or gas jet. The invention of the electric light revolutionised the magic lantern, making it safer and more compact. Nevertheless lanterns continued to be ungainly until the evolution of the slide projector after World War Two. Also worth looking out for are the old-fashioned large glass slides with scenic photographs, fairy tale pictures or the words and music of popular songs, used in days when community singing was all the rage.

Mangle boards

Wooden boards used for wringing out clothes after washing and rinsing. Before the advent of the clothes-mangle with rotating rollers operated by handle, mangle boards were used to beat the excess moisture out of one's washing. These boards may be found all over Europe. In an age when the women of the community congregated on the banks of a stream to do their laundry it was inevitable that they should vie with each other in the sumptuousness of their mangle boards. These objects lent themselves ideally to decoration which usually took the form of intricate carving. Like apple scoops, distaffs and wooden spoons, dealt with elsewhere in this book, mangle boards were often carved and decorated by young men and presented as love-tokens to their sweethearts. There were traditional patterns associated with particular districts, or the universal symbolism associated with love and romance. They date from the Middle Ages down to the present century and may still be made in the more remote districts of Eastern and Central Europe.

Mauchline ware

A type of decorated wood ware named after the Scottish town of Mauchline, Ayrshire, where it was chiefly produced. Small boxes of all kinds were made of Scots planewood and painted, usually on the lids but sometimes on the sides also, with flowers, country scenes or famous local landmarks. Subsequently transfer prints of scenery or sporting subjects were applied and varnished over. This distinctive craft seems to have originated in the Kincardineshire village of Laurencekirk in the eighteenth century and spread in the early nineteenth to Mauchline, Auchinleck, Cumnock and other villages of central Ayrshire. Not surprisingly Robert Burns and characters from his works, such as Tam O'Shanter and Soutar Johnny, were favourite subjects of Mauchline ware. By the late nineteenth century, however, such manufacturers as W. and W. Smith of Mauchline were also decorating boxes with scenery in other parts of Britain and these were eagerly collected by tourists as souvenirs from Land's End to John O' Groats. An offshoot of the pictorial boxes was the tartan box which became popular in the early nineteenth century as a result of Sir Walter Scott's romantic revival of Highland dress. Snuff-boxes, stamp-boxes, boxes for pins, trinkets and pills, needle-cases, wood-based pin cushions and even work-boxes may be found in Mauchline ware.

Meat cleavers

In these days of pre-packed foods in supermarkets the average house-wife has little or no use for the old-fashioned meat cleaver. As the use of deep freezers spreads, however, and the idea of buying half a sheep, if not half an ox, catches on, the meat cleaver could make a come-back – though I suppose there will always be the obliging butcher to do the heavy work. Meat cleavers may be recognised by their heavy broad blade, often perforated at one side so that they could be suspended from a hook for safety reasons when not in use. A whole collection of cleavers might be somewhat frightening, but one or two make interesting orna-ments for the kitchen wall, in company with other culinary tools and implements.

Meat jacks

Instruments which preceded the invention of the electric rotisserie in modern kitchens. The meat jack was a clockwork device which rotated slowly and enabled meat suspended from it to be roasted evenly over an open fire. Meat jacks were invariably made of brass which was kept highly polished when not in use. They make intriguing and attractive ornaments for a cottage in the country, and are now one of the more popular lines in rural antique shops.

Military chests

This form of travelling furniture developed during the Napoleonic Wars and enjoyed a vogue in military circles down to the end of the nine-teenth century. They were produced in two parts which could be placed end to end and used as a bed. They may be recognised by the flush-fitting drawer handles, brass-reinforced corners and carrying handles mounted at either end. Occasionally the top drawer was fitted as a writing desk; this type is highly desirable. Until recently there was little demand for such chests but now they have been rediscovered by trendy interior decorators, and large quantities have been exported to America in the past decade, pushing up their market value considerably.

See also Travelling Furniture.

Mineral water bottles

Rubbish tips and waste sites are the major source of supply of old mineral water bottles. Even in these days of standardisation there are still a few individualistic styles about, the Coca Cola bottle being the best known. But consider the evolution of the 'pop' bottle over the past 150 years and you will appreciate the range of shapes and patent sealing devices which have been used in that period. The problem facing the manufacturers was how to prevent the gases from escaping. The earliest solution was to use corks and, in the manner of sparkling wines such as champagne, to store the bottles on their sides so that the cork was kept moist and expanded to fit tightly. To ensure that the bottles were stored on their sides they were shaped with pointed bottoms so that it was impossible to stand them upright. William Hamilton patented his 'egg-shaped' mineral water bottle in 1814 and this remained in use into the 1870s when other devices superseded it. In the last quarter of the nine-teenth century such refinements as the screw stopper (1872), the marble stopper (1875), the swing stopper (1875) and the crown cork (1892) revolutionised the fizzy drinks market. Apart from the sealing devices great individuality was expressed in the size and shape of the bottles. Before the era of 'coke', mineral waters and soft drinks were usually limited to one locality, so a search up and down the country will reveal an astonishing variety of brands and types.

Strong Chests for Travelling.
(Of good seasoned wood.)

Zinc Lined Chests.
(Recommended for Officers' use and for India)

Mote skimmers

More than a century ago, and well before the invention of tea-bags, floating tea-leaves were a source of considerable irritation. Not only were tea-leaves much larger and coarser than they are nowadays but the tea invariably included bits of twig and other foreign bodies, to put it delicately. In order to remove this flotsam from the surface of the tea-cup the mote skimmer was invented. Silver spoons with their bowls perforated in intricate patterns served this purpose. Generally speaking the more decorative specimens are later, usually Regency or Victorian. Instead of a handle with the usual flattened end there was a spike, for dislodging blockages in the spout of the tea-pot. Larger versions, usually in copper, brass or tin-ware, were in use from medieval times for skimming the scum off the surface of soups and stews. Though more functional in appearance they also were decorated with patterns of holes to some extent. The brass and copper examples, in particular, look attractive when brightly polished.

Moustache cups

The wearing of moustaches in western European society was fashionable from the mid-1850s to the 1920s. It began with the Crimean War and went out with World War One. In the intervening period of almost seventy years the 'moustache movement' gave rise to a minor industry which produced special combs for grooming the whiskers, and a branch of ceramics specialising in a type of cup which prevented the moustache from being unduly soaked. Moustache cups can be identified by the segment across one side of the rim. When the cup was raised to the lips this segment came against the moustache and protected it from the liquid. Moustache cups were popular in Europe and America and every pottery manufactured them at some time or other, so that they may be found in different kinds of pottery and porcelain and exhibiting a wide variety of decoration.

82

Muffineers

Like the caster (q.v.) this device was used as a sprinkler; only in this case powdered spices were involved. They were indispensable in elegant households for the serving of muffins at tea-time. These hot-buttered cakes were eaten with salt, pepper and grated cinnamon and it was the last-named which was dispensed in a muffineer. Generally speaking the difference between a caster and a muffineer was one of size, the latter being smaller. Another distinguishing feature was that the holes were finer. The earliest muffineers resembled pepper-pots but as the eighteenth century progressed they became taller, with a pedestal foot, baluster-shaped body, and tall, narrow domed lid. They were produced in silver, sometimes with porcelain body, and were often gilt-lined. They reflected the various styles of silver from the reign of Queen Anne to early Victorian times when they gradually went out of use.

Music covers

The use of lithography in printing sheet music in the early nineteenth century stimulated a distinctive art form. Not only was it possible to print the musical score in this way but greater flexibility enabled the publisher to embellish the cover with an attractive picture which no doubt helped to sell the music. Illustrated music covers were in existence from the early seventeenth century, produced from wood-blocks or engraved copper-plates. With the advent of chromolithography (printing with different coloured inks) about 1840 the illustration gradually increased in size until it occupied the entire front cover, with the title, inscriptions and imprint superimposed. It has been estimated that between 1820 and 1900 over 100,000 different examples of illustrated music covers were produced in Britain alone. The illustrated sheet music of Victorian times was the equivalent of today's pop record. It was not uncommon for the most popular songs to be printed in editions of 250,000 or more. The zenith of the illustrated music cover was between 1840 and 1870, between the introduction of colour and the adoption of mechanisation in printing. After 1870 standards deteriorated rapidly. During the heyday of music covers, the publishers employed printers of a very high standard, the leading companies being M. and N. Hanhart and Stannard & Dixon. Individual artists whose work is now highly prized include Alfred Concanen of Stannards and John Brandard of Hanharts. The subjects depicted on the covers ranged far and wide. Collectors of militaria, for example, will find numerous examples featuring army and naval items.

Mustard pots

The seed of the black mustard plant (*Brassica nigra*) has been used as a table condiment in Europe for 2000 years. In earlier times it was prepared by immersion in hot water which produced oil of mustard. About 1720, however, a Mrs. Clements of Durham hit upon the idea of grinding the seed in a mill and sifting the resulting flour. Subsequently, Americans began preparing and selling bottled mustard in the form of a thin paste mixed with vinegar and spices. To the collector, mustard pots mean two different things – the receptacle in which the mustard is retailed and the container used on the dining table. In the former class came a variety of bottles and stoneware jars dating from the end of the eighteenth century. Many of them are impressed or decorated with the name of the manufacturer and some are highly ornamented with fancy lettering and floral motifs. Traditional stoneware jars are still used for French mustard. Table mustard pots were manufactured from the early eighteenth century onwards, usually of silver with a characteristic glass lining to prevent chemical action of the mustard on the precious metal.

Napkin rings

Rings for holding napkins, or serviettes as they were once known, have been around for more than two centuries. Those families who were sufficiently genteel to use napkins at meal-times could generally afford silver rings, hence this was the most popular material from the early 1700s right down to World War One. All the famous silversmiths, from Paul de Lamerie and Hester Bateman to Paul Storr, manufactured napkin rings, which thus offer one of the few opportunities to collectors of modest means to acquire a piece of silver by one of the 'greats'. Individual items or sets are highly collectable, especially if the decoration is unusual. Many examples which can be found today bear the crests of aristocratic families. Others were engraved with inscriptions commemorating christenings, silver wedding anniversaries and so on. Materials other than silver became popular in the late nineteenth century. Bronze rings in sets depicting different landmarks are worth looking out for. Other sets commemorated the Columbian Exposition, the Paris World's Fair of 1900 and similar events. They have also been produced in ivory, painted or carved wood, glass or porcelain.

Nutmeg graters

When spiced drinks such as hot toddy and mulled wine were popular the nutmeg grater was in common use. This was a small box or cylinder containing a grater on which the nutmeg was ground. These graters may be found in wood, ivory or bone, but the more elegant examples were made of silver or Sheffield plate and it is these which offer the greatest scope to the collector. They were produced in various fancy shapes – nuts, urns, eggs and cones being the commonest. The majority of the silver graters date from 1760 to 1850.

Office equipment

Elsewhere in this book are separate notes on blotters, erasers, ink pots and stands, letter openers, pen-wipers, paper clips, paperweights, pencil sharpeners, staple fasteners, string boxes and typewriters. But there are many other collectable objects from the office of years ago. The Victorian love of the ornate was extended to the most utilitarian items of office equipment : filing cabinets, letter racks, desks and swivel chairs may all be found with lavish ornamental scrollwork. Fortunate the 'lady typewriter' of Victorian times who wore long skirts; her modern mini-skirted counterpart would be for ever laddering her tights in such baroque surroundings. Junk shops and second-hand stores are a fruitful source of old office equipment, much of which is not only serviceable but an attractive contrast to the streamlined décor of modern offices.

Oilcans

Oilcans dating from the late nineteenth century were produced in many different shapes and sizes, depending on the purpose for which they were intended. They were made in steel, tin-plate, copper, brass or nickel-plate. Some look very attractive when well polished. Others were brightly painted and bore the name and trade-mark of the manufacturers. Engineers' oilcans were often made in matched sets of five or six in different sizes for different purposes. They ranged from the large cans with long spouts used by locomotive engineers to the tiny oilcans used for clocks and sewing machines. The tiniest examples often consisted of circular glass phials attached to a fine brass or bronze spout. The larger copper or brass oilcans are now popular in America as flower and plant-holders.

Padlocks

These hanging locks derive their name from the medieval foot-pads or highway robbers. The padlock, used to secure the boxes and baggage transported in wagons and on horseback, was supposed to be secure against foot-pads. Locking devices are thought to date back to 2000 B.C. and it is believed that padlocks are also of great antiquity. Just as tremendous improvements were made in locks generally in the mid-nineteenth century so also the padlock developed in the form used today. Self-locking, spring-loaded padlocks were patented in 1897 but long before that date there were many interesting types which appeal to the collector with a mechanical mind. Several different shapes were used, the shield being the most popular, and examples can be found in which the ornamentation resembles a heraldic escutcheon. The drop plate covering the key-hole was often decorated with fine engraving. Padlocks came in all sizes, from the miniatures used to secure jewel boxes or dog collars, to the giants used on doors and trunks. Tiny padlocks in silver or gold and often embellished with pearls or precious stones were sometimes used to secure necklaces. Even the more utilitarian padlocks of seventy years ago could boast a wide range of ornamentation.

Paper clips

The insignificant piece of bent wire which serves nowadays to hold sheets of paper together is very different from the highly ornate device used in the 1890s. The large paper clips of eighty years ago – often measuring up to four inches in length – were unlikely to be discarded or misused in the way the modern clips so often are. With their massive springs and fearsome spikes they conveyed an impression of solidity and durability. Some may be found embellished with the figures of birds and animals, or shaped in the form of a pair of hands or clam-shells. Others had geometric or floral decoration, and there were even paper clips decorated with the symbols of societies and organisations. Paper clips symbolising good luck were made in the form of horse-shoes. The clips were usually manufactured from steel, sheet brass or copper. More rarely they may be found with silver or gold plating, or with enamel or glass decoration incorporated in their design. These elaborate paper clips gave way to the more utilitarian bulldog clips and wire clips before World War One and they are now increasingly hard to find.

Paste jewellery

If ever there was a misleading term it is paste jewellery. There is nothing 'pasty' about it and it is, in fact, a form of glass produced over the past 2000 years in imitation of precious stones. As such it has long been popular in the manufacture of jewellery, but it has had other applications also. The carved hardstones of classical times – agate, jasper, onyx and chalcedony – were successfully imitated by James Tassie in his glass paste cameos of the eighteenth century. Paste or *pate de verre* has also been used in the manufacture of snuff and scent bottles, trinket-boxes and small ornaments. The chief use of paste in the nineteenth and twentieth centuries, however, was in jewellery. The highly convincing amethysts and emeralds of today's costume jewellery are the direct descendants of the glass beads of earlier generations. Many of these baubles can still be picked up quite cheaply. The glass used in jewellery enjoyed many names as fancy as the colours and textures achieved – the schmelzglass of Germany, the lythyalin of Bohemia, the peach blow and amberina of America and the purple slag of England.

Pencil sharpeners

The earliest mechanical contrivances for sharpening pencils were of the type designed for desk use. They were relatively complicated and cumbersome, and many ingenious devices were incorporated in them to ensure efficiency. They operated on one of two principles. In one type the pencil was placed inside a roller lined with sandpaper and rubbed to a fine point by the rotation of the roller. In the other type a cutting wheel was used. Like their modern counterparts these desk sharpeners had a box attached to collect the shavings and graphite dust. Inevitably the boxes were subject to the lavish decoration fashionable in the late nineteenth century and it is in the variety of the ornamentation that the appeal of these pencil sharpeners lies. Small pencil sharpeners designed for the pocket evolved in the 1890s and consisted of small steel tubes containing a cutting blade which could be adjusted by means of screws. These sharpeners differed little from the type in use to this day.

Pen-wipers

Small pads of cloth for cleaning pen nibs were popular around the turn of the century and remained in use until the fountain pen, with its self-cleaning nib, did away with the necessity. Although any old rag would suffice for the purpose, it was inevitable that the late Victorians and Edwardians, with their love of the ornate, should invest the pen-wiper with a touch of fanciful decoration. Elaborately decorated covers were produced in leather or embroidered cloth. Some even had wooden, metal or glass mounts embellished with pictures or attractive patterns. Others had an ingenious sponge top which could be moistened for easier cleaning.

Pickle jars

As examples of late nineteenth and early twentieth century glassware become more desirable (and consequently more expensive) it is worth considering the mundane items in this material. Surprisingly enough the pickle jar possesses many features that recommend it to the collector. These jars come in many different shapes and sizes and although they were usually manufactured from clear or greenish bottle glass they were seldom plain. Examples may be found with attractive moulding, particularly on the stoppers, and there are jars with quite intricate pressed-glass decoration on their sides. Since these jars were often used and re-used on many subsequent occasions they are seldom found nowadays with their original labels intact. Such rarities are highly prized by connoisseurs of food-store ephemera. Sometimes, however, jars with metal lids bore the manufacturer's name or advertisement thereon, while others have the maker's inscription stamped on the base.

Pictorial book-bindings

An important landmark in the publishing world was the introduction of wholesale binding by the publisher of books prior to sale. This practice began about 1822 and was well established by the beginning of the Victorian era, as an alternative to the paper wrappers in which books were issued as a temporary expedient before being bound to the customer's taste. Cloth on board became very popular and by 1840 had virtually ousted the traditional methods of binding in Britain and America. From the collectors' viewpoint edition bindings held comparatively little interest until recently, but now an increasing number of collectors are turning their attention to the bindings of Victorian and early twentieth century books. This was a period of great ingenuity in book-binding; embossed bindings, papier mâché bindings and even bindings which simulated wood carving were patented in the decade before the Great Exhibition of 1851. Around the middle of the century gift and prize books appeared in an astonishing array of bindings with panels of vellum, silk, tortoiseshell, wood and even porcelain. Bindings became increasingly pictorial, usually reproducing in gilt or silver die-stamping one of the plates or scenes referred to in the text. Towards the end of the century metallic designs gave way to pictures die-stamped in various colours. Pictorial bindings died out in the 1920s as dust jackets gradually came into use.

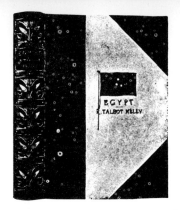

Pill-boxes

In the era before the advent of the National Health Service people were more likely to resort to patent medicines and do-it-yourself cures for ailments than they are nowadays. This was the heyday of some weird and wonderful 'medicinal compounds', to judge by the extravagant claims made for them by their promoters, not only in the newspaper and magazine advertisements of the period but in the lavish embellishment of the boxes in which they were retailed. Patent medicine bottles are comparatively scarce, though just as collectable; presumably there was a deposit on the bottle, refundable on return, on account of the cost of glass. Boxes, on the other hand, were a relatively inexpensive form of packaging and could therefore be discarded. More likely, however, they were hoarded for years on end. From time to time people unearth surprising quantities of old pill-boxes in the attics of hypochondriacal relations. Their labels are often a testimony to the lost art of ephemeral printing and graphics. The pills themselves should *not* be collected. Unknown chemical compounds seldom grow old gracefully or safely. At one time there was a tax on patent medicines and many of these old pill-boxes will be found bearing a revenue stamp by which they can be dated fairly accurately. A surprising number of these pills were either laxatives or abortifacients, or both, judging by the claims on the labels.

Pin cushions

Although pins themselves are not used as widely as they formerly were, the cushions which housed them are attracting considerable attention from collectors. The majority of pin cushions were made of plush or velvet stuffed with straw, horsehair or similar material. They were often circular, oval or rectangular, but examples can also be found in fancy shapes – cats, dogs, birds, flowers, vegetables, or human figures (especially angels or cupids). Other pin cushions were mounted in metal or porcelain objects – shoes, hats and houses. Allied to pin cushions are pin holders. These were circular, not unlike small yo-yos in appearance, with strips of felt or padding between two discs. These pin-holders may be found in lacquered wood, marquetry or in the wood mosaic known as Tunbridge ware.

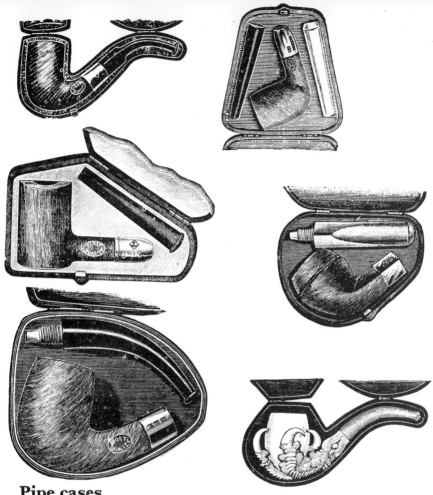

Pipe cases

In an age (1600–1850) when clay pipes, especially the slender church-warden, were popular the pipe case was necessary to protect the pipe from damage while it was being carried around. Thus cases made of wood with cloth linings were devised. The earliest cases were of plain wood, fashioned in two halves with hinges on one side and clasps on the other. Gradually they became more intricate, with slim, tapering shutters on the underside and lavish carving on the outside and particularly the part which covered the pipe-bowl. The more expensive cases had silver inlays or were mounted with finely carved ivory figures. Those cases with a separate hinged compartment for the pipe bowl date from the second half of the eighteenth century when a knob was fitted to the foot of the bowl so that it could rest on the table. Elaborate pipe cases were a speciality of Germany, the Low Countries, France and Austria. Those produced in England and America were generally much plainer.

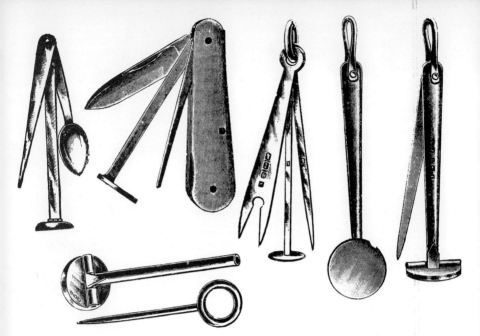

Pipe-stoppers

Occasionally one will come across a small object which, at first glance, appears to be a letter seal, but the fact that the business end is quite plain indicates that some other purpose was intended. These objects, their handles often highly ornamented, are pipe-stoppers, used by pipe-smokers to tamp down the tobacco in the bowl. The purpose of the stopper was to keep the tobacco reasonably tightly packed in order to produce the correct amount of 'draw'. Since techniques in smoking have not altered it is a mystery why pipe-stoppers should have declined in popularity. Pipe-smokers today use various unsatisfactory substitutes, such as a pencil stub or even their finger tips. Pipe-stoppers were in use from the early seventeenth century till about 1850. The earliest ones were whittled from wood or bone, and these materials continued to be used until the 1840s. Better quality stoppers were elaborately carved in ivory and these are now among the most highly prized. Whalebone, mother-of-pearl and various kinds of shell were also used, though such materials were relatively scarce. Among the other non-metallic substances sometimes encountered are glass, earthenware and porcelain. The favourite medium for pipe-stoppers was metal. Brass was most popular and the majority of the ornamental stoppers in antique shops today were produced in this alloy. They were also made in copper, bronze, lead, iron, silver or gold. Some were mounted with tiny figures, often of contemporary personalities, some were shaped like human legs, others had coins or medals mounted in the handle.

Player-pianos

These are pianos fitted with a mechanical device for automatically play-ing written music or for reproducing the playing of a pianist. The principle underlying this device is the difference between internal and external air pressure. A roll of paper with holes punched in it is rotated against a tracker bar in such a way that the piano action can be operated. Various companies in the United States at the turn of the century produced player pianos. The best known of these were Pianola, Ampico, Angelus, Duo-Art (Aeolian) and Welte-Mignon. They went out of fashion before World War Two and examples in reasonable condition can be picked up relatively cheaply, though the appropriate rolls of music are becoming hard to find.

Pounce boxes

A type of caster (q.v.) used on the writing desk rather than the dining table. In the days before blotting paper, fine sand was sprinkled over a letter to dry the ink, the unabsorbed sand being tipped back into the box. The name is derived from the fact that the box was pounced or punched with holes through which the sand was sprinkled. This type, distinguished by the relatively large holes, was in use from the end of the eighteenth century when surfaced paper was introduced. Prior to that, however, the pounce box was used to sprinkle powdered gum sanderach, not so much to dry the ink but to add 'body' to the very porous rag paper then in use. These boxes had holes of a much finer gauge. Pounce boxes were made in silver, brass, copper or pewter and were often produced with matching inkstand and inkwells.

Powder compacts

This term is used in Britain to describe that *sine qua non* of the ladies' handbag or purse. In America these items are known as dorine boxes or vanity cases (to add to the confusion, in England a vanity case is a large box on a lady's dressing table containing all the paraphernalia associated with her make-up!). By whatever name they are known these handy objects were indispensable to the well-groomed woman by the time of World War One. They were made of metal, either circular, oval or square, with tight-fitting lid, and contained a small mirror, cake of face powder and small powder-puff. Nowadays face powder is often sold in plastic compacts and metal compacts are somewhat less popular, but from 1910 to 1950 the decorated compact had its heyday. They were made of silver or gold, often richly jewelled or inlaid with enamel, and represented the acme of the silversmith's craft. For the mass market, however, there were numerous fine examples in silver or gold plate, with *guilloche* engraving. Others were mounted with paste or ivory cameos and these are well worth looking out for.

Printed boxes

Biscuit boxes (q.v.) are the best known examples of the printed tin box which has been popular in Europe and America since the 1820s when tin-plate came into use as a form of packaging. Pot-lids and pomade-tops have long been collected on account of their decorative qualities, but the humbler tin box has been largely ignored. Yet this is a fertile field with infinitely greater scope. Apart from biscuit tins, perhaps the best known and most enduring of this *genre*, there are chocolate boxes, candy boxes, cigarette tins, boxes for shortbread and sweetmeats, as well as all manner of non-perishable goods. The decoration of these boxes in multicolour lithography enabled almost any subject to be depicted – pretty girls, scenery, flowers, famous people and historic events. The boxes can be collected according to subject, or according to the purpose for which they were made. Many of the boxes intended as gifts were produced in unusual designs – animals, birds, hearts, bundles of books, rustic cottages or clocks. The printed tin box is virtually the only form of decorative packaging used today that is worth preserving on aesthetic grounds.

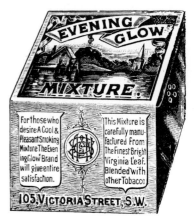

Printed handkerchiefs and headscarves

These souvenirs of places and events have a surprising antiquity, dating back to the late eighteenth century when copper plate engraving was first applied to textile printing. The invention of the Perkins Bacon rose-engine in 1819 and the repeal of the taxes on imported cotton and calico in 1831 greatly stimulated the printed cloth industry. While printing was already utilised for curtains, drapes and soft furnishings its application to small decorative items was quickly realised. By the mid-nineteenth century printed silk or cotton squares were being produced in large quantities depicting scenery, sporting events and contemporary personalities. As the century progressed the political and patriotic aspects of printed handkerchiefs resulted in the souvenirs of the Crimean and Boer Wars, the Golden and Diamond Jubilees of Queen Victoria, the exploits of Garibaldi, the inauguration of American presidents and other events both national and international. The agitation for Irish Home Rule and women's suffrage was also recorded by printed handkerchiefs carrying a political message. Improved techniques in recent years have led to a whole galaxy of souvenirs in textile form. A modern variant is the printed tea towel decorated with recipes and household hints, maps, tourist resorts, landmarks and almost anything under the sun.

Prisoner of war work

In one sense the handicrafts of prisoners of war have long been known and appreciated by collectors and high prices are paid for the intricately carved bone sailing ships and straw marquetry produced by the Frenchmen incarcerated at Norman Cross and Dartmoor during the Napoleonic Wars. Apart from the ships, with their plaited hair rigging and metal work fashioned from seamen's ear rings, there were trinket boxes, model forts and churches, automata, dolls and fans. The basic materials were cattle bones, odd scraps of wood and straw, the last named being employed painstakingly to build up elaborate mosaic and marquetry patterns to decorate the lids and sides of boxes. But prisoners from other, more recent wars have also contributed their quota to this brand of folk-art and, as yet, their work is little recognised or valued. I well recall how German and Italian prisoners during World War Two supplemented their meagre wages by their arts and crafts – wood-carving and poker work being especially popular. One wonders where all these ash-trays, work-boxes, and carved figures of thirty years ago have disappeared to.

Purdoniums

A purdonium is a type of coal-scuttle invented in the nineteenth century by a Mr. Purdon. Its distinction lies in its rectangular shape and close-fitting lid, designed to prevent coal-dust from escaping. Inside was a plain tinware container for the coal. The lid, sides and handle of the purdonium were usually embellished with brass fittings cast in ornamental shapes while the body itself was japanned. Elegant purdoniums of the late nineteenth century are quite plentiful and in little demand (thanks to central heating). One type of purdonium had the opening at the top and the lid upholstered so that it could be used as a stool as well as a receptacle for coal.

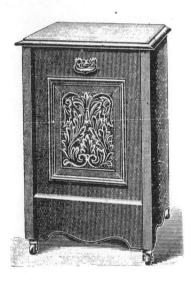

Pyrography

The fancy name for pokerwork, the art of decorating surfaces (usually wood or bone) by burning with heated tools. At its worst this manifests itself in cheap wooden plaques which are the backbone of the souvenir mass-market. Whether these items will ever attain antiquarian interest and value is open to doubt. Pyrography, however, has been practised as a folk art all over the world for an extremely long time and inevitably a large number of pokerwork articles are worth collecting. European artists of the eighteenth and nineteenth centuries, for example, brought the technique to its peak by the subtle use of different tools applied to the surface for varying lengths of time and intensity. In this way they achieved pictures of great depth and form, with a wide range of shading from light brown to black. This art died out in the second half of the nineteenth century, or rather became debased since it is still widely practised. Other substances which have been given pyrographic treatment include horn, ivory and even leather, for the tourist trade in many parts of the world.

Quaichs

The Scottish Gaelic word *cuach*, meaning the hollow inside of a bird's nest, gives us the term for a distinctive type of shallow drinking cup much favoured in the Highlands for the imbibing of whisky. Characteristic features of quaichs include a wide shallow bowl, often set on a circular foot, and two handles projecting at right angles on either side of the top. The quaich in medieval times was carved out of a piece of wood but by the early 1600s it was being produced in turned woodware and a subsequent refinement was the use of silver for the handles, rim and foot. Later still the interior of the cup was lined with silver and by the beginning of the nineteenth century these vessels were being made entirely in silver, lavishly decorated with thistles and Celtic ornament in the fashion of the romantic revival. Most of the quaichs now found in Scottish antique shops belong to this category. Occasionally pewter was used but these and authentic examples from an earlier generation are rare outside museum collections.

Rack plates

Decorated, often commemorative, plates for display on the racks above the dresser were popular from the late seventeenth to the mid-nineteenth centuries. The early examples, in faenza, maiolica or tin-glazed delft-ware, are very expensive nowadays. They include the William of Orange plates popular in England after the revolution of 1688 and the *istoriato* plates fashionable in Italy a century earlier. Plates bearing the names of parliamentary candidates and political slogans were a speciality of the Bristol delft manufacturers in the eighteenth century. Long after electioneering plates went out of vogue political events continued to be a fertile subject for rack plates. Nautical themes were another perennial favourite in Britain, and the railway boom of the mid-nineteenth century also inspired a wide range of pictorial plates. Though they declined in popularity at the end of the nineteenth century rack plates continued to be produced for outstanding royal events such as Victoria's jubilees of 1887 and 1897 and the coronations from 1902 to 1953. In the past decade, however, commemorative or pictorial rack plates have enjoyed a tremendous revival and are now produced to celebrate all manner of events.

Ring trees

Occasionally one will come across objects in porcelain, metal or wood with a circular base and a branched trunk standing about six inches high. These objects were designed a century ago for rings, at a time when the wearing of valuable rings was more common than it is today and fashionable ladies could not be content with only one or two. The majority of these ring trees were functional in appearance, with a plain vertical rod and branches at right angles. Some fancy types were produced in the shape of an upraised hand or in the form of a stag's antlers. A relatively late type consisted of a tapering metal rod on to which the rings were impaled. The snag with this kind of ring tree was that if you wanted a ring at the bottom of the pile you had to unthread all the others. Another ring stand from the turn of the century had a circular metal ball with hooks radiating from it, on which the rings were hung.

Safety lamps

It is amazing how several minds will independently come up with a startling invention more or less simultaneously. In 1818 George Stephenson, the railway engineer, noticed that the flame of the candle did not pass through the small apertures of the latticed fender. From this observation he devised a safety lamp with a gauze wire aperture and tested it satisfactorily at Killingworth Colliery near Newcastle-upon-Tyne. He was subsequently awarded a silver tankard filled with 1000 guineas as the discoverer of the safety lamp. At the same time, however, it transpired that Sir Humphrey Davy had been working on the problem of safe illumination in coal-mines. In his lamp the flame was entirely surrounded by fine mesh gauze. Dr. W. Reid Clanny also devised a safety lamp at the same time, using a glass cylinder with a gauze top. Flame safety lamps of the Davy type have been used in collieries and mines all over the world for a hundred and fifty years, though the flame lamp has declined in recent years in favour of the electric lamp. The flame lamp served not only as illumination but as a test for the presence of gas or fire damp. Rewired for electricity, the old safety lamps are finding a new occupation as table lamps, with polished copper and brass work.

Salt and pepper sets

Condiment sets consisting of a pair of small containers for salt and pepper came into use in the nineteenth century. At an earlier period salt pots were small vessels (usually of silver with blue glass liners) and pepper-pots or mills were quite separate articles. The advent of table salt and the refinement of powdered cayenne pepper popularised the salt and pepper set. The objects were often identical in every respect but for the different perforation of the tops, although sometimes they were designed in fancy shapes which complimented each other. Thus small male and female figures have long been popular subjects for these condiment sets. The range of novelty shapes and types is enormous and every material from wood to porcelain, from metal to plastics, has been used. They are still being produced, and no doubt will continue to appear as long as food requires seasoning.

Sand buckets

Excellent examples of decorative tinware are the children's sand buckets which first became popular at the end of the last century. Nowadays they have largely been superseded by plastic buckets. From the collector's point of view the most attractive buckets were produced in the period up to World War One. Thereafter standards of finish and decoration deteriorated as sand buckets were turned out by the million for the mass market. The earliest examples had relatively staid floral designs but by Edwardian times gaily coloured seaside scenes showing children at play were becoming popular. Often the miniature spades were decorated with matching motifs. For the nostalgic, who recall the palmy days when a trip to the seaside was a real treat – and not marred by the traffic jams of today – these old-style sand buckets will bring back happy memories. Like any other container of suitable capacity these sand buckets are now being adapted as pots for house-plants. But beware of loose seams and holes in the bottoms if you use these buckets for plants requiring frequent watering.

Sand pictures

Benjamin Zobel, a German artist who settled in eighteenth century London, was the leading exponent, if not the inventor, of the sand picture and was even patronised by the Court as well as the nobility and lesser gentry. The basic picture would be outlined on card or wood, covered with adhesive substance and sand of different colours carefully sprinkled on the appropriate place. Animals, scenery and landmarks were the most popular subjects but portraits and even reproductions of Old Masters were occasionally produced. The sand picture developed in the early nineteenth century as a kind of folk art and was particularly popular in the seaside resorts of the English south coast. Alum Bay, in the Isle of Wight, was a source of many different coloured sands and this explains why many of the scenes depicted in sand pictures are from that island. Zobel and his family produced sand pictures on a commercial basis, but the art was also practised as a modest cottage industry throughout the nineteenth century.

Scales and balances

This is a subject with enormous scope, ranging from tiny pocket scales once used for checking the true weight of gold coins to elaborate cast-iron weighing machines. Pocket coin balances often consisted of simple brass devices with a weight at one end and a circular pan at the other designed to hold sovereigns or half sovereigns. More intricate were the balances which folded neatly into a slim wooden case which could be carried conveniently in the pocket. Examples of these coin balances are known from the seventeenth century, though most of the surviving types are probably of later vintage. They were very necessary in the bad old days before coins were given a grained edge and dishonest individuals were in the habit of chipping slivers of gold off the edges. Apothecaries' scales may also be found in small, collapsible pocket sets, complete with brass pans and range of weights. Letter balances were introduced in the 1840s when mail began to be charged according to weight instead of by the number of pages and the distance conveyed. These balances often have contemporary tables of postal rates engraved on them – a useful way of dating them. Other types of weighing device include early spring balances, scale beams, hanging scales, counter-top scales, grocers' balances and coin-operated weighing machines. In many cases the weights themselves are eminently collectable.

Baby Balance.

103

Scrimshaw work

Scrim-shouting or skrim shander, the alternative names for scrimshaw, denote a type of folk art which is wholly American. The New England whalers of the seventeenth and eighteenth centuries originated the art of engraving on whale bone or whale's teeth. Nautical subjects – ships and whaling incidents – were naturally the most popular, but human and animal figures and primitive heraldry were also common. Sometimes, too, the tusks of walrus and narwhal were similarly decorated, the tusks being fashioned into useful articles such as napkin rings, pastry crimping-wheels and even clothes pegs. Whale bone stay busks were often lavishly decorated with scrimshaw work and presented as a token of affection. The idea of engraving on bone or similar substances spread inland and accounts for the powder horns decorated with hunting scenes or battles from the Anglo-French colonial wars in America. The art died out about 1830, though in the more remote areas it lingered on until the beginning of this century. Examples of scrimshaw work have long been keenly sought by collectors in America, though not readily appreciated in Britain or Europe until recently.

Sealed glassware

A wine bottle with a glass seal impressed on its side was an English idiosyncrasy and, judging from extant examples, was particularly prevalent in the West Country. The seals were usually about an inch in diameter, embellished with dates, initials and occasionally coats of arms or even portraits. Thus wine bottles can not only be dated but assigned to specific owners, ranging from inns to the colleges of Oxford and Cambridge, from tradesmen to members of the aristocracy or civic corporations. Sir Kenelm Digby is said to have invented the glass bottle as a container for wine, in place of the wooden cask or leathern jack. The date of this invention is assigned to 1632. Within twenty years seals were being impressed on the bottles. Seals inscribed RW, attributed to Ralph Womersley, were discovered in excavations at Williamsburg, Virginia, and since he died in 1651 it is assumed that seals were in use by that time. The earliest dated fragment is known from 1652. Most examples of sealed bottles belong to the eighteenth century and they had gone out of use by 1840, though they have been revived by certain vintners in recent years as a form of trade mark. Since 1970 seals have been applied to commemorative goblets to commemorate the *Mayflower* 350th anniversary and the demise of sterling coinage. A penny of King Offa in glass form was impressed on tankards marking the latter event.

Sewing birds

Devices for holding cloth securely to a sewing table while it was being embroidered were known as sewing birds, presumably since they were often in the form of a bird which gripped the material in its beak. Similar gadgets have been seen in the shape of butterflies, animals or human figures – but they are still known as 'birds'. They were usually made of iron or brass with a clamp fitted to the base so that they could be anchored to the table. Others were made of wood with metal fitments and a few of the late nineteenth century examples were produced in silver plate. Some of the more elaborate sewing birds incorporated pincushions or contained compartments for needles, thimbles and cotton.

Sewing machines

In 1755 Charles Weisenthal invented a double-pointed needle with the eye in the centre. This was adapted by Thomas Saint in 1796 for his machine capable of quilting, stitching and sewing. The first practical sewing machine was invented by a French tailor, Barthelemy Thimmonier in 1836. The earliest Thimmonier machines were ungainly wooden affairs but in 1848 he perfected his invention and secured patents in Britain and America. In 1834 an American, Walter Hunt, produced a lock-stitch machine, but failed to patent it. Twelve years later Elias Howe patented a machine with a curved eye-pointed needle and under-thread shuttle. This formed the basis for the machine patented in 1851 by Isaac Merritt Singer. Although numerous refinements and variations appeared subsequently the Singer machine of 1851 embodied all the principles on which modern sewing machines operate. By the end of the nineteenth century sewing machines were being produced in large numbers. They were built to last, and proof of their sturdy construction is the number which survive to this day. They range from tiny portables, in wooden carrying cases, to the large table models and the treadle-operated machines which were still being manufactured up to World War Two.

Shoe horns

Devices for easing the foot into the shoe have been recorded over many centuries. For hundreds of years the commonest types were (and still are) made from curved strips of cow-horn, hence their name. Later, wood was found to be an acceptable substitute and in the late nineteenth century brass or steel became popular. Inevitably some form of decoration was applied to the upper end or handle of the shoe horn, either by carving directly on to the horn or wood, or by means of silver mounts. Decorated shoe horns were fashionable in the era of 1880–1910 and many different types can be collected today. Like buttonhooks (q.v.) shoe horns were often given away to customers by shoe shops. Examples of these bearing the name or trade mark of the shop are worth considering as early examples of 'special offers' and sales promotion gimmicks.

Slot machines

These are such a twentieth century phenomenon that it seems incredible that they have, in fact, been in existence for 2500 years – almost as long as coins themselves. The earliest record of a slot machine is that used in Egyptian temples in the pre-Christian era. A coin inserted in a slot triggered a simple mechanism which released the appropriate amount of holy water. Nevertheless, until the advent of regular coinage of standard weight, thickness and diameter in the seventeenth century, the automatic vending machine as we know it today could not be evolved. Among the earlier types of coin-operated device were mechanical toys at side-shows and music boxes or nickelodeons in public houses – the ancestor of the modern juke box. Slot machines or one-armed bandits, paying out from two to two hundred coins depending on the combination of symbols rung up, have had a chequered career (see Gambling Equipment) though are now generally accepted as respectable. Coins are used to operate all manner of devices, from haircream dispensers to pay-telephones, from stamp machines to laundromats. A device affixed to the doors of public lavatories has even given the English language a monetary expression for a basic bodily function.

Soap boxes, dishes, stands and brackets

Numerous different kinds of receptacle have been produced in the past century for soap and many of these are worthy of the collector's attention. The most interesting are those in earthenware or porcelain and all the famous potteries seem to have produced them at one time or another. Soap dishes and boxes have also been manufactured in glass, and though less interesting than their ceramic counterparts these may sometimes be found in the art glass which was fashionable (particularly in the United States) at the turn of the century. Metal soap containers were produced in brass or copper with silver or even gold linings. Others had a glass or porcelain lining with a silver outer case and in the more expensive examples cast or chased ornament would frequently be lavished on the lid and sides. Soap stands were made of pottery, porcelain, glass or metal (brass or nickel-plated steel). The soap was placed on an inner stand, pierced with holes to allow the water to drain away. Soap brackets, affixed to the edge of the bath, were usually more functional in appearance, made of wire, but examples in fretted brass or silver-plate with decorated edges have been noted.

Spectacles

The spread of literacy after the invention of printing stimulated the use of spectacles and a trade devoted to their manufacture developed in northern Italy and southern Germany during the sixteenth century. A portrait of Cardinal Ugone painted in 1352 depicts him with two mounted lenses of glass fixed in front of his eyes, proving that spectacles in a rudimentary form were known in the late Middle Ages. The optician emerged as a professional craftsman by 1600 and there was a Spectacle Makers' Guild in England by 1629. The London opticians enjoyed a reputation for the best spectacles in Europe, after Marshall's improvements in the grinding of lenses were introduced between 1690 and 1693. The best of the London spectacle makers in the early eighteenth century charged as much as sixteen guineas for double-jointed standard gold spectacles, complete with gold case. Monocles became fashionable about the same time. Bifocals were first produced about 1760, Benjamin Franklin being an early customer. Horn or leather were the earliest materials used as mounts, but steel, silver or gold became popular by 1650. Early examples of spectacles are scarce, but interesting types from the nineteenth century onwards are still reasonably plentiful.

Standishes

Another name for an ink-stand (q.v.) said to be derived from the words 'stand' and 'dish'. This name was popular in the eighteenth century and has been retained to describe desk-stands of the Georgian period. The earliest examples were, in fact, wooden or metal dishes or trays which stood on writing tables. They were divided into compartments for ink-pots, pens, pounce-pots (q.v.) and pen-knife. The later and more elaborate types were raised on ornamental feet and were decorated in the prevailing baroque, rococo or Regency styles. Usually they were rectangular, but one sometimes finds circular or oval standishes. The term 'inkstand' gradually came into use about 1850 when separate ink-bottles, rather than the sunken ink wells, were incorporated in the design.

Staple fasteners

Gadgets for securing sheets of paper were patented in the late nineteenth century. Although the principle on which they operate has not materially altered in the past eighty-odd years the appearance of these fasteners has changed enormously. In the days before World War One staple fasteners could be purchased with elaborate silver bases and tops. Enamelled metal fasteners gaily decorated with pictures were also popular fifty years ago and are worth looking out for.

Stools

Most books on furniture neglect or completely ignore the humble stool. Lowly in appearance and regard, it is nevertheless an object of great interest, reflecting the various changes in fashion, materials and techniques of craftsmanship. If you want to possess an article of Jacobean furniture, for example, there are still sufficient examples of sturdy foot-stools from this period at a reasonable price. Country antique shops are the best source of supply; for some inexplicable reason stools seem to have been more popular in farms and country houses than in town mansions. The more elegant, upholstered stools, particularly of the eighteenth and early nineteenth centuries, are relatively expensive, but bargains abound in the robust country varieties. This is a facet of furniture which tended to vary less from generation to generation and more from district to district, as a hunt through the antique shops of Scotland, Wales and the West Country will reveal. Range farther afield, to New England, Scandinavia or Italy, and the variety of stools increases enormously.

String boxes

Otherwise known as twine-holders, these objects were once considered indispensable in shops and offices, but have all but been relegated to the scrap-heap since the advent of adhesive tape. They consisted of circular drums with an aperture through which the string passed. They may be found in a wide variety of materials. The wooden ones often exhibit fine carving and woodturning on the domed lid. Comparatively rare are the boxes made of papiermâché, lacquered to a high glossy finish. Metal boxes, of copper or bronzed steel, are usually more utilitarian in appearance, though they may occasionally be found with die-stamped decoration on the sides or with painted or enamelled ornament. Some of them were fitted with circular feet or elaborately scrolled legs. Others had a ring fitted in the top of the lid, so that they could be hung from a beam or post. Apart from the domed drum the most popular shape was the bee-hive. Relatively scarce are string-boxes made of earthenware or glass.

Stud boxes

Studs or collar buttons became necessary in the mid-nineteenth century when stiff collars and neckties replaced the stock and cravat of an earlier generation. Small boxes, usually circular or oval, were designed to house these studs. They were made of leather, ivory, silver, silver-plate or even porcelain. While many were frankly utilitarian, quite a number were highly decorative. There were also novelty boxes in unusual shapes or with studs mounted on the lid, accompanied by some suitable inscription such as 'A friend in need is a . . .', or 'Here's your . . .'.

The advent of collar-attached shirts for all but the most formal occasions has led to a decline in the use of collar studs and the stud boxes have now joined the ranks of the obsolete and the antique.

Stuffed animals and birds

The skins of animals have been preserved by hunters for centuries, but it is only from the sixteenth century onward that attempts were made to stuff the skin and create a lifelike representation of the animal. The oldest example now extant is a crocodile in St. Gall museum, Switzerland, dating from 1627. The early stuffed beasts had a soft toy look about them and it was not until the middle of the nineteenth century that the science of anatomy was applied to the art of taxidermy; Jules Verraux of Paris being the pioneer of a more realistic approach, which was then adopted by Professor Henry A. Ward of Rochester, New York. Many of the world's museums obtained their stuffed specimens from Ward's Natural Science Establishment between 1860 and 1890 and the art spread to Britain and other European countries at this time. In the late Victorian period it became fashionable to have cases of stuffed animals and birds. Changing fashions and the growth of conservation programmes led to the decline of this form of ornament. In recent years, however, Victorian or Edwardian cases of stuffed animals and birds have returned to fashion, though not much effort has been made to revive the taxidermy business, due to the prevailing climate of conservation.

Sugar tongs

The production of granulated sugar in cube, loaf or tablet form dates from the early years of this century. Thus the tongs associated with bowls of cube sugar did not make their appearance until shortly before World War One and did not become popular until much later. The majority of examples manufactured in the past fifty or sixty years are in electro-plate or stainless steel and of little potential interest to the collector, but fine examples in silver are worth considering.

Tape measures

Small tape measures, usually in thirty-six inch or one metre lengths, were produced in metal or tortoiseshell cases around the turn of the century. It is not so much the measures themselves but their cases which are of interest. They may be found in various novelty forms – beer barrels were one favourite. Others were made of brass or silver and highly ornamented as was the custom of the period. A popular motif showed a house with its yard full of children at play. The caption to this scene – 'A Full Yard' – may seem feeble by present-day standards of humour, but, judging from the prevalence of this tape measure, it must have delighted the tailors and seamstresses of seventy years ago. Another 'novelty' was in the form of a straw boater, with the inscription on the crown 'Most hats cover the Head, this covers the Feet'. A few tape measures of the pre-World War One era were made of celluloid, while ivory or porcelain cases are not unknown though seldom seen nowadays.

Thermometers

In 1714 Gabriel Fahrenheit, a German instrument-maker living in Holland, invented the thermometer and gave the world a name which was in common use until recently. Fahrenheit used a slender glass column of mercury and this has been the basic principle of the thermometer ever since. Thermometers have much in common with barometers (used for measuring atmospheric pressure) but have not enjoyed the same degree of popularity with collectors – all the more surprising when it is realised that nineteenth and early twentieth century thermometers were often highly decorated. This is especially true of the wall thermometers used to measure room temperature. They were mounted on polished wood bases decorated with carving and moulding and are every bit as collectable as barometers. Others had oval surrounds of white enamelled metal decorated with floral motifs or animal figures. Some even struck a cultural note, incorporating portraits of Shakespeare and other literary personages. Thermometers designed to stand on mantel-shelf or table-top had ornamental stands, with gilded rococo metal work or tiny figures of dogs and horses.

Theatre playbills and programmes

One of the most important branches of ephemera is that pertaining to the theatre and vast collections of playbills and programmes have been formed. Bram Stoker, better known as the creator of Dracula, was secretary to Sir Henry Irving and in this capacity was able to make a fine collection of playbills at the turn of the century. Posters and playbills advertising plays, revues and other theatrical entertainments date from the eighteenth century and are interesting examples of the different styles of typography used at various periods. More compact, and in many respects more interesting, are the theatre programmes. These are more recent than playbills, dating from the mid-nineteenth century and gradually becoming more elaborate with pages of supporting advertisements and potted biographies of the principal actors and actresses. Particularly desirable are programmes from first nights. Playbills and programmes can be collected in various ways – according to the theatre, or pertaining to the works of particular playwrights, or tracing the career of a particular actor. There are now several specialist dealers in this subject and the market is rising steadily, but literature on theatrical memorabilia is scanty as yet.

Tie pins and scarf pins

Pins for securing items of dress have been in use for thousands of years, ranging from the fibulae of Roman times to the safety pins of the present day. In between, from the eighteenth century onward, come the decorative pins used at different times to secure dresses, scarves, shawls and neck-ties. These pins were much smaller than hat-pins (q.v.) but were subject to similar decorative treatment. A large collection of these pins could be formed, with ornaments grouped thematically – animals, flowers, insects, good-luck symbols, civic emblems, college fraternity badges and semi-precious jewels. Around the turn of the century such pins were often sold in sets with a uniform style of ornament.

Tinsel pictures

These wall decorations were popular from about 1850 till 1930 and numerous examples turn up in jumble sales and church bazaars even now. The earliest ones are thought to have evolved from the toy theatre figures – penny plain, twopence coloured – of mid-Victorian times. It became a popular pastime to decorate these figures with tinsel stars and ornaments. Thus many of the surviving tinsel pictures have a theatrical motif, Shakespearean characters being a favourite subject. Gradually, however, the idea was extended to include topical personalities, sporting celebrities and members of the Royal Family. At the same time tinsel pictures were being manufactured in their entirety and became somewhat stereotyped. By the turn of the century they had taken on the familiar form of a figure in silver paper against a black background. Ladies in crinolines and gentlemen in stovepipe hats superseded the Royalty of an earlier period. The monotony of these later tinsel pictures was their downfall. There has been a revival of the art in recent years, and a return of the variety of subject and treatment seen in the earliest examples. Tinsel, silver paper, foil wrapping and even milk bottle tops are now used to make exciting montages.

Tipstaves

Rods of wood or metal which were formerly carried by law officers as a mark of their authority. At one time the tipstaff was the identifying feature of the village constable and served both a ceremonial and a defensive function. As a rule these tipstaves were ornamented with the royal coat of arms or the arms of the borough or county. English tip-staves were usually of ebony with brass mounts and a small metal crown at one end. Minor differences in the heraldic details of the royal coat of arms are useful in dating these staves. In general the later examples were more functional and less ornamental in appearance. The use of tipstaves died out about 1850, though they lingered on for a further generation as part of the equipment of inspectors in the Metropolitan Police. Tipstaves were also carried by minor functionaries such as inspectors of the poor, bank officers and borough surveyors and examples may be found with the name of the office and town or district inscribed on them.

Toasting forks

Yet another example of the kitchen implement (q.v.) which can be used for ornament. Toasted bread, tea-cakes and muffins have long been popular and there was something special about toasting the bread over the open fire at tea-time. Consequently every household, however humble, had at least one toasting fork. From the collector's viewpoint the best examples are those with openwork decoration, wrought metal tines or shafts and ornamental handles. Usually they were produced in wrought iron, but brass or bronze were also popular. Toasting forks went out of use in comparatively recent times with the introduction of grilles and electric toasters and the disappearance of the open fire.

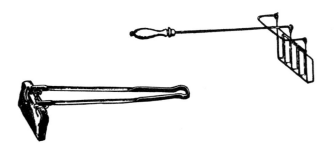

Toilet sets

Chamber pots (q.v.) are often collected as individual items, but complete sets comprising wash-basin, ewer and matched pair of pots are also worth watching out for. Sometimes as many as seven separate items might comprise a toilet set, and include soap-stand, toothbrush stand and tooth-glass holder – all in matching earthenware or porcelain. Complete sets are now comparatively scarce, though the tenacious collector will often be able to pick up matching items, with a bit of luck and patience. These sets date back to the mid-nineteenth century and survived till about 1930, though the increasing use of water closets and bathrooms in all but the most remote rural areas led to their decline. At the same time the wash-stands which contained these sets are worth considering. They had a marble top and a cupboard underneath for storing the 'crockery' when not in use. Many of these stands have been chopped up and their tops re-ground and converted into coffee table tops.

Tools and implements

You may call a spade a spade, but have you ever thought of collecting it? With the development of folk museums in recent years, implements of the farm and garden have acquired antiquarian status. Country antique and junk shops are a rich hunting ground for all manner of agricultural tools long cast aside with the advance of automation. Flails and rakes, peat-cutters and foot-ploughs, butter-churns and milk-maid's yokes are among the objects worth looking for. At the other extreme there are the tools of many trades and professions, some rendered obsolete by advances in techniques, some merely old-fashioned versions of instruments still in use. An idea is to collect historic examples of tools associated with your own vocation. Draughtsmen, dentists, doctors, scientists and engineers will be able to collect antiquated items connected with their profession in much the same way as soldiers, both serving and retired, pursue militaria. An advertisement in the appropriate professional journal will often yield items of collectable interest.

Trade tokens

Unofficial coins produced in many countries at various times during a shortage of government coinage. In Britain they were produced on three main occasions – in the seventeenth century, from 1787 to 1797 and from 1804 till 1817. Token halfpence and farthings were issued by tradesmen and inn keepers prior to the coinage reform of 1672. Between 15,000 and 20,000 different types were issued. Technically, most of these early tokens were crude, often bearing no more than the date and initials of the trader. A few, however, had ambitious designs showing civic coats of arms. Very few base metal coins were struck in Britain between 1755 and 1797, although it was not until 1787 that the Parys Mine Company of Anglesey began minting halfpennies and pence with the effigy of a Druid on the obverse. The practice rapidly spread throughout Britain and countless thousands of tokens were produced. Many of these later tokens were of the highest technical excellence and latterly whole sets were issued mainly for sale to collectors, with pictorial motifs, political symbolism and heraldry. The regal coppers of 1797 brought the need for tokens to an end, though there was a brief resurgence of tokens, in silver this time, during the Napoleonic Wars. Tokens have been produced in the United States during the Civil War (1861–65) and in many European countries during and after World War One.

117

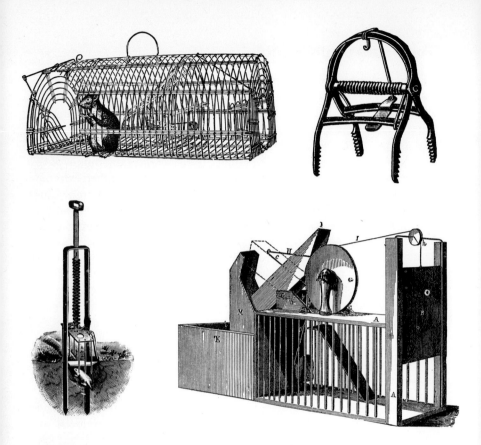

Traps

Not, at first sight, a pleasant subject – and yet traps have been produced all over the world, in all ages, for every kind of animal, including man himself. The collector of treen (woodware) or farming implements will probably come across various kinds of traps for snaring birds and small animals such as rabbits, hares, foxes and weasels. But quite an interesting collection could be devoted to domestic traps designed to catch rats and mice. Many of these gadgets were highly ingenious, embodying gates, tunnels and cages to contain the victim, or devices for choking or de-capitating the unfortunate beast. Some traps sold in the late nineteenth century were multiple traps, allegedly capable of snaring several animals simultaneously. Traps with such evocative names as the Delusion, the Improved Rat Killer, the Holdfast, the Break-back or the E-Z Katch Trap were popular seventy years ago and examples still turn up from time to time. Fly traps with wire or glass cages were also popular in late Victorian times, before the advent of the arsenical fly-paper or fly spray.

Travelling furniture

This is a class of furniture which has received little attention, but is worthy of consideration by the collector. Already military chests (q.v.) are in great demand. The sea-chests popular at one time with sailors are also beginning to attract attention. They may be recognised by the numerous little compartments set into one or more of the sides or the inside of the lid. Unlike the military variety they seldom possessed drawers, and were always made as a single item, not in two halves. Various types of collapsible furniture came into use in the late nineteenth century when big-game hunting and expeditions to remoter parts of the world became popular. Camp-beds, chairs, stools, and wash-stands, designed to be folded or dismantled for easy transportation, were more robust and cumbersome than the flimsy tubular aluminium furniture of the present day. They were often fine examples of the cabinet maker's art and are just as deserving of attention from collectors as the more permanent furniture of the period. The best travelling furniture was produced in the era 1880–1920.

Folded.

ASHANTEE HAMMOCK.

Trays

This is such a vast subject that the would-be collector may wish to specialise in one aspect of it. Perhaps the most interesting facet is the use of trays as an advertising medium. This practice seems to have begun in America in the 1890s and spread to Europe early this century. Metal trays are indispensable in public bars and it was inevitable that the breweries should have been the first to use trays to promote their beer. Beer trays decorated with emblems, trade marks and slogans are almost as limitless in scope as the beer mats and ashtrays which are a popular feature in bars and beer-halls the world over. Soft drink manufacturers, to a lesser extent, have also produced advertisement trays – Coca Cola, Pepsi Cola and Schweppes being among the best known. Tobacco companies and manufacturers of confectionery have provided some notable examples of tray art, using multicolour lithography to reproduce famous paintings or depict scenery. Other trays portrayed film stars and beauty queens, popular heroes and international celebrities, so there is enormous scope for thematic collections. Electroplated tea and coffee trays in many styles and shapes have survived from the late nineteenth century but unless their decoration is exceptional they lack the human interest of the advertisement trays.

Trivets

As examples of wrought iron work trivets have a great deal to commend them – they are small, relatively inexpensive, and useful. For those who still have open fireplaces, even if central heating has been installed, a fine wrought iron trivet set with logs can be quite an attractive feature. Other trivets which may be encountered are the small triangular ones on which flat-irons (q.v.) were stood, and the circular types for standing coffee pots.

Truncheons

Weapons carried by policemen and security guards; historically they follow the same pattern as tipstaves (q.v.) with which they are sometimes confused, though they differed in length. Truncheons range from simple sticks to thick, barrel-shaped clubs. A refinement was the articulated truncheon which acted like a flail when swung. Early truncheons, like tipstaves, were lavishly decorated with coats of arms and mottoes. The more interesting (and collectable) examples also include the names of constabularies and police forces. Those used by the Metropolitan Police in the mid-nineteenth century were carried in leather scabbards attached to the officer's waist-belt. These truncheons, complete with scabbard, are now comparatively rare. The use of truncheons spread to other parts of Britain in the nineteenth century and ornamentation continued as late as 1920 in some districts, thus offering a rich field to the collector. Less decorative, but interesting nonetheless, are the truncheons and night sticks used by American and European police forces.

Typewriters

Although a patent was taken out as early as 1714 by Henry Mill, an English engineer, for 'an Artificial Machine or Method for the Impressing or Transcribing of Letters', the first practical typewriter to be constructed was that devised by William Austin Burt of Detroit in 1829. Four years later a Frenchman, Xavier Progin, invented the type-bar principle which is used in most typewriters down to the present day. Charles Thurber of Worcester, Massachusetts, produced a machine in 1843 incorporating the longitudinal movement of a platen – another feature of the modern typewriter. Dr. Samuel Francis of New York invented a machine in 1857 which closely resembled a grand piano in size, but at least established something approaching the typewriter keyboard system! Ten years later Christopher Sholes, Carlos Glidden and Samuel Soule of Milwaukee produced the first typewriter as we know it. Sholes persevered and within two years had evolved a further thirty machines. In 1873 Sholes and Glidden signed a contract with the gunsmith E. Remington. The Remington machine, which went into production the following year, remained basically unchanged until 1928. Soon rival companies were producing machines on either the type-bar or type-wheel principle, the latter system, long discarded, having made a recent come-back in the latest electric typewriters. The era from 1880 to 1914 provides the widest variety of different types, some more weird than efficient.

Umbrella stands

Stands for umbrellas were popular from about 1850 to 1920 but have gradually slipped into disuse since then. The reason is hard to find, since umbrellas are as necessary today as they were fifty years ago. Perhaps a trend away from cluttering porches and hallways has something to do with it. At one extreme are the large stands made of wrought iron with a metal tray at the foot to catch the water from dripping umbrellas. Though many of these objects are unlovely and ungainly, others display fine examples of wrought iron decoration and have a ready appeal to collectors of decorative ironwork. Some of these were additionally painted or gilded and are rather attractive. At the other extreme, however, are the simple cylindrical stands, about twenty-four inches high. These may be found in earthenware, bronze, brass or steel. The ceramic ones often had decoration in the Chinese blue and white style, or underglaze transfer prints of flowers and landscapes. Popular relics of World War One are brass shell cases converted as umbrella stands. At one time these were quite plentiful but few of them seem to be around today.

Verre eglomise

This term denotes a process of decorating glass by drawing and painting on the reverse side of the glass and then backing the decoration with metal foil, usually in gold or silver leaf. The style is derived from the work of the Parisian artist and print-collector Jean Baptiste Glomy who lived in the second half of the eighteenth century. Glomy is credited with inventing a method of framing prints with black and gold fillets, painted from behind the glass. The term *verre eglomise* has been debased and has often been applied loosely to any form of glass picture involving painting on the reverse side. However, the process of metal foil backing is of far greater antiquity, having been recorded in the Middle East, whence it was introduced to Italy at the time of the Renaissance. This type of decoration was widely practised in France in the seventeenth century and was introduced to England by Huguenot artists in the 1680s. Individual pictures in verre eglomise are comparatively scarce, though still surprisingly undervalued, and are sometimes found in junk shops, their true worth unrecognised.

Waffle irons

Waffles are little known in Britain, but are a popular delicacy in America. They came originally from the Low Countries and Germany a century ago. Small batter cakes served with maple syrup are still holding their own as a breakfast food – despite the increasing popularity of cereals of the snap, crackle, pop variety. Waffles are baked in a special utensil which takes the form of two blades with their opposing surfaces raised, indented or pierced in various patterns. Though many waffle irons are relatively plain, others bear quite intricate patterns and it is this feature which endears them to the collector. The older examples, of course, were often lavishly decorated about the handles in the prevailing fashion of the late nineteenth century.

Walking sticks

Most people these days would be content with a stout ash stick but such is the wide range of types of walking stick manufactured during the past three centuries that a fine collection could be assembled for a reasonable outlay. They range from the distinctive 'country' sticks in blackthorn or ash, to the elegant ebony canes with gold or silver heads carried by fashionable gentlemen up to about 1914. Associated with walking sticks are sword sticks, cane sticks and single sticks which could be used as weapons. A comparatively rare type was the walking stick which incorporated an air gun – a device favoured by poachers as a discreet firearm. Walking sticks, rather than rattan canes, were carried by officers in Highland regiments and many of these were mounted with regimental badges. Particularly desirable are those bearing small commemorative plaques in silver for presentation purposes.

See also Canes and Cane Handles.

Wallpaper

The use of paper as a wall covering became popular in the seventeenth century, gradually ousting cloth tapestry. The custom originated in China and the earliest wallpapers were imported to Europe by the East India companies. They set the tone for the European wallpaper of the eighteenth century, which often had Chinese motifs. They were printed in black from wood block engravings. Other colours were gradually introduced and by the beginning of the nineteenth century lithography and copperplate engraving were adding to the variety of wallpaper. Mid-Victorian developments included the use of heavy embossed papers and paper with surfacing simulating other materials, such as cloth or velvet. The French developed the mural wallpaper in which several rolls would be joined together to make a single picture, usually a landscape. By the 1870s, wallpapers had become lavish in the extreme, with heavy floral patterns or repeating motifs of hunting scenes. As a reaction against these florid styles William Morris and his colleagues in the Arts and Crafts Movement began designing wallpapers with more restrained naturalism. It is amazing how much old wallpaper has survived. Scraps and remnants were often used to line trunks or drawers and a search through attics and boxrooms will usually bring to light some interesting examples.

Watch stands

Gadgets designed to hold pocket watches when they were not being worn. Usually they stood on the bedside table at night. From the mid-eighteenth century to World War One, when pocket watches were most fashionable, these stands were produced in large numbers. Some were functional in design, with an aperture so that the face of the watch remained visible. Others were in the shape of trees so that the watch could be suspended from one of the branches. Similar stands, incidentally, were provided for rings and often known as ring trees (q.v.). Watch stands were manufactured in silver, bronze, brass, wood and even porcelain. Those made in the late eighteenth century sometimes had rich ormolu gilding and intricate decoration. Such watch stands are rather expensive nowadays, but there are plenty of nineteenth century examples to provide a large collection of different types.

Watering cans

The watering cans in use today are usually plain galvanised steel with little aesthetic appeal. A century ago, however, they were manufactured in copper or brass and examples of these, highly polished, make attractive ornaments or plant holders for the sun lounge or conservatory. Around the turn of the century watering cans in tinplate were painted on the outside and decorated with gay transfer-printed pictures of flowers or garden scenes. Unfortunately the hard usage to which they were subjected meant that these lithographed decorations are seldom found in pristine condition, though the popularity of these floral watering cans in America has encouraged a minor industry in refurbishing and redecorating them for use as plant-pots.

Whips

As collectors' pieces they have surprising scope, though one always suspects at least an element of the sado-masochistic in those who collect whips. They range from the elegant riding crop to the fearsome *sjambok* popular in South Africa. By an odd coincidence both the *Sunday Times* and *The Observer* of July 11th 1971 ran stories concerning a type of whip known as a bull's pizzle. The *Sunday Times* story began with a reference to an advertisement in *The Times* of July 7th from a dealer wishing to purchase such a whip. A bull's pizzle, it explained delicately, 'is what even the most genteel suspected'. Any farmer whose bull died would, in the old days, cut off the organ and hang it from a beam in the barn. A weight would then be fastened to it so that it stretched to a length of about forty inches. The weight would be given a twist, so that the pizzle acquired a cork-screw effect. In reply to the advertisement Christie's said they had three, while a lady in Belgravia offered one for £12. *The Observer*'s story concerned a fire-arms dealer in Essex who recently discovered a batch of pizzles in a Madrid military store where they had lain for at least a century. The pizzles came from fighting bulls and were once used to whip the horses in gun-teams. Interest in pizzles seems to be world-wide. *The Times* advertisement was inserted on behalf of a Japanese collector; the Essex dealer reported an enquiry from someone in Bermuda who was apparently writing a book on the subject!

Whistles

Although man is capable of emitting as loud a whistle by his own efforts as any other animal, it seems that artificial whistles have been made for thousands of years. Whistles in terra cotta or bronze are known from prehistoric times and wooden whistles have probably been in existence just as long. Nor was mankind content with purely utilitarian devices. Fancy shapes in human or animal form were always popular. From the seventeenth century onwards elegant whistles in silver or gold, decorated with enamel and precious stones, were produced as playthings for the wealthy, and these objects of vertu have long commanded high prices in the salerooms. However, for the collector of modest means, the scope is enormous. Military and police whistles, decorated with coats of arms and insignia are sought by militaria enthusiasts – as are also the bosun's pipes which were the naval counterpart. The development of tinplate in the nineteenth century led to the appearance of penny whistles which could play a full octave, or novelty whistles die-stamped in all kinds of shapes. There are also children's toothbrushes, pens and pencils and even cutlery with built-in whistles.

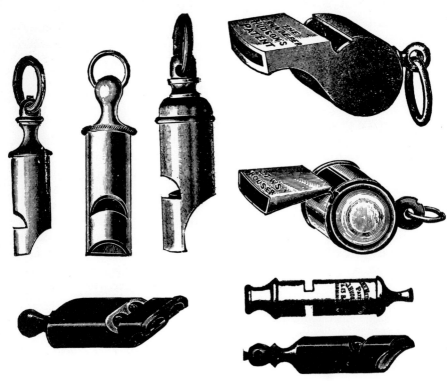

Wicker furniture

Furniture woven from reed, willow, rattan or cane was popular in America and Europe from about 1870 till 1920 or even later. Unlike wooden furniture (which could be chopped up for kindling) there was little that one could do with wicker furniture when it had outlived its usefulness or gone out of fashion. Consequently it was often relegated to the attic or out-house – to be unearthed generations later. There has been a revival of interest in wicker furniture in recent years and a certain amount of it is being manufactured today. But there is also plenty dating from the end of the last century which is perfectly serviceable. Chairs, sofas and tables in wicker-work rise steadily in value as the demand increases. They can either be left in their natural state or painted, and they blend very well with the relatively simple décor of modern homes. One may even find wicker-work lampstands and plant-pot holders.

Window display pieces

It is difficult to say precisely when sales techniques came to be applied to the merchandising of goods, but probably by the beginning of the nineteenth century brightly coloured cards and even three-dimensional objects were being used in window displays of goods. Some of these early 'eye-catchers' seem crude and whimsical by the sophisticated standards of the present day, but in their very naïveté lies their charm. Simple mechanical devices, operated by clockwork, were coming into use by about 1850 and by the end of the century automatic figures capable of working up to five hours on a single winding were common. They took the form of animals or people whose hands, legs, heads and even eyes moved in order to gain the attention of passers-by. These display pieces were made of card, wood or (more rarely) sheet metal. Modern examples from shop windows include enlarged or miniaturised models of the product, illuminated signs and sales dispensers. Also worth considering are the objects found in public bars to advertise various brands of beer, wines and spirits.

Wooden measures

With metrication imminent in Britain, hastened along by entry to the Common Market, the traditional units of measure will become a thing of the past. School children will be glad to substitute the litre and the cubic centimetre for the bewildering array of gills, quarts, gallons, bushels and pecks, but with their passing something colourful will have gone out of our lives. I anticipate that, in a wave of nostalgia, collectors will turn to old weights and measures with renewed interest. Particularly worth looking for in country junk shops are the old wooden measures used by farmers for measuring grain and vegetables. They ranged in capacity from the gill (cupful) to the Imperial bushel. A complete set of measures would be a rarity these days, but odd examples turn up quite frequently. The small ones were made of strips of wood bent into a circle nailed to a round wooden base. Bands of copper or brass enclosed the measure and add to the attraction of measures when highly polished. The royal cypher was branded into the tin and this mark is a useful guide to the date of the measure. The larger measures make attractive holders for plant pots.

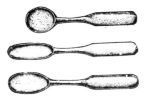

Wooden spoons

'Spoons' was a nineteenth century popular expression to describe a courting couple, and the word 'spooning', synonymous with courting, is still sometimes used. The words derive from the age-old custom of exchanging love tokens in the form of carved spoons. The practice has survived as a tourist gimmick in Wales (most of those now sold in Welsh souvenir shops are machine-made rather than hand-carved), but old Welsh loving-spoons, with their distinctive double head, still turn up from time to time. Actually the custom of giving a carved wooden spoon to one's sweetheart was widely practised throughout Europe and exists to this day in parts of Spain, Brittany, Switzerland and southern Germany. The handles were finely carved with traditional love symbols, but the more elaborate examples were engraved with landscapes, animals and human figures. As well as carving and engraving, painting and pokerwork were employed in their decoration. Dates, names or initials were often worked into the design.

Writing sets

In addition to ink-pots and ink-stands, already mentioned, writing sets are worth considering as collectable items. Some are merely ink-stands of a more elaborate appearance, incorporating a tray for pens and pencils and perhaps a rack for letters and postcards. Others have tiny drawers and compartments for seals, stamps, sealing wax, paper clips, erasers and other writing paraphernalia. Though the majority of writing sets were static objects designed to sit permanently on a desk others were intended to be portable and were housed in attractive wooden or leather cases. The compendium, with its pad of note paper, envelopes and blotter, is the modern counterpart of the portable writing case, and although most of these tend to be strictly functional nowadays a few are still being produced which possess great aesthetic appeal and are likely to interest future collectors.

Zarfs

The proper name for Turkish coffee cup holders – and a much neater term than 'Turkish coffee cup holders', by which they are more commonly known. The cups themselves were made without handles and the zarf was intended to protect the drinker's hand from scalding. Zarfs were produced in the bazaars of the Near and Middle East and fashioned in brass or silver, often intricately decorated or inlaid. In the mid-nineteenth century, however, there developed in France and Switzerland a minor industry in zarfs for export to the Levant. The European zarfs were noted for their delicate enamelling and gilding. Such objects were shown at the Great Exhibitions of 1851 and 1862 and the Exposition Universelle of 1867. Zarfs of a less pretentious type are produced to this day in the Balkan countries and Turkey, but mainly for the souvenir market.

The Garnstone Press can also provide

Antique Maps

P. J. Radford

An Introduction to Lace

Gabrielle Pond

An Introduction to Small Antiques

James MacKay

The U.S. Mint and Coinage

Don Taxay

Coin Collecting for Grown-up Beginner

James MacKay

Not forgetting

The Country Gentlemen's Catalogue
1894